Presented To:

_____

From:

_____

Date:

_____

Warrior for Revival

Warrior for Revival

The Life Story & Principles of Philip Mantofa

Philip Mantofa and Ribkah M.H.

DESTINY IMAGE® PUBLISHERS, INC.

P.O. Box 310, Shippensburg, PA 17257-0310

"Speaking to the Purposes of God for This Generation and for the Generations to Come."

This book and all other Destiny Image, Revival Press, MercyPlace, Fresh Bread, Destiny Image Fiction, and Treasure House books are available at Christian bookstores and distributors worldwide.

For a U.S. bookstore nearest you, call **1-800-722-6774**.

For more information on foreign distributors, call **717-532-3040**.

Reach us on the Internet: **www.destinyimage.com**.

ISBN13 TP: 978-0-7684-3873-4

ISBN 13 HC: 978-0-7684-3874-1

ISBN 13 LP: 978-0-7684-3875-8

For Worldwide Distribution, Printed in the U.S.A.

1 2 3 4 5 6 7 8 9 10 11 / 13 12 11

Dedication

PHILIP Mantofa's boldness and conviction were born in the depths of his mother's heart. These traits make him who he is and help explain the Lord's calling on his life.

The support and example of his father taught him to be a humble and patient servant of the Lord. The attention, tears, and prayers of his loving parents gave this ordinary man the courage to overcome his weaknesses and become a chosen man of God. For these reasons, this book is dedicated to Hardi Mantofa and Suzanna Lindawati, Pastor Philip's mother and father.

May this book not only raise up a generation of young people who fear the Lord, are dedicated to the Church, and fervent in their calling, but also inspire parents to become examples like these two. Amen.

Table of Contents

Foreword

WHO would have thought that an ordinary man, full of weaknesses, and relatively young, would win 100,000 souls for the Lord? Yet God raised up Pastor Philip Mantofa to bring unprecedented waves of revival to the young people of Indonesia. Mawar Sharon (Rose of Sharon) Church, where he ministers, has planted 70 local churches all over the country. The number increases as God continues to move. Raising up young people to reach their own generation is a new phenomenon for many. Most of these young people never intended to carry out a huge task for the Lord. But today, because of the faith of one man, hundreds of youth are preparing to become missionaries around the world.

Pastor Philip follows in the Teacher's footsteps. In his mind, nothing is more beautiful or important than his relationship with the Lord Jesus Christ, the great Teacher. He will never exchange this intimacy for anything the world has to offer. He does and always will follow in His steps, trusting Him as Lord and sovereign Ruler.

When Pastor Philip put his faith in the Lord, his Creator, the Lord made a way for his ministry. In the beginning, it was not as easy as he had thought it would be. Many sharp stones wounded him and obstructed his path. His progress toward success was not paved with applause and the sound of praise. Often he was forced onward tearfully. But he never turned aside or avoided the path the Lord had chosen for him. Because of his persistent faith and dedication, many people have been touched by the anointing and power on his life and his intimacy with the Holy Spirit.

Pastor Philip's perseverance has borne fruit. The example of his life and faith has moved many to boldly accept their calling, despite the risks.

Pastor Philip's life has inspired many people. A great number of leaders and representatives of their generation say that he is the instrument God used to help them find their glorious call as leaders who share their lives and give opportunities to others. By the example of his life and commitment to Jesus, he has co-labored with God in the fields ripe with harvest to mold ordinary men and women into obedient, determined, and powerful soul-winners for their generation.

Warrior for Revival narrates the events of his life and the principles of his ministry. This book was written to raise up a generation of young people who are not yet 30 to demonstrate the character of Christ and be used by God in mighty ways—a generation that will make the devil and his kingdom tremble. Above all, *Warrior for Revival* is the story of an ordinary young man, full of weaknesses, who seeks and finds the Lord Jesus Christ, the Ruler of his soul. The Holy Spirit empowers his ministry today.

Each chapter in this book begins with my narration and interviews of the many lives Pastor Philip has touched. Pastor Philip wrote the concluding sections, which set forth the principles he lives by.

I hope the story of Pastor Philip Mantofa's life and faith will inspire you and bless your ministry. Amen.

Ribkah M.H. (Sianne)

Preface

IN these last days, many young people are frittering their lives away. They seem to think that youth is not the right time to invest their lives in the Lord, that there will always be another tomorrow to start living with purpose. Youths now are known to live without identity, principles, or goals. Many Christian youths are no exception.

As a young man, I am called to declare to my generation to begin their spiritual walk now—not tomorrow. The primary reason this book was written is to show the world that it is not impossible for a young person to live for Christ. All the testimonies in *this book*, which Sianne wrote, happened before my 30th birthday.

Some people think I've reached the peak of my ministry. I believe just the opposite. I never considered myself successful. I see everything that has happened so far as God's preparation for me to do greater things for Him in years to come. All I've done so far is to get a successful head start so I can reach the finish line as soon and as perfectly as possible (see 1 Cor. 9:24-27).

In the years since I repented and received His call, God has accomplished many awesome and extraordinary works through my life and ministry, which I share in this book. Although these works have seldom been achieved by young people my age, that doesn't mean I've "arrived." Rather, I am persuaded that all any servant of the Lord can do is to surrender to God and become a vessel through whom He can work. Any power and anointing people see in my life is not mine, but His.

I hope the Lord will use not only me, but that He will use my spiritual children even more. I know God does not use everyone in the same way, but as long as He uses me, at least my disciples will have an example that will push them to find their own mantles of anointing. That is the reason this book was written. I hope my life story and principles will inspire you.

His servant,
Pastor Philip Mantofa, BRE.

Prologue

I VISITED the home of Pastor Philip Mantofa's parents to learn about his beginnings. How could I cowrite a book about this young man's extraordinary life unless I knew how it first began?

As I entered the home office, Pastor Philip's father, Hardi Mantofa, was busily cutting paper at his desk. By the desk were neat rows of books and framed family photos—the wedding pictures of his three sons, and a family gathering in Canada. Suzanna Lindawati, Pastor Philip's mother, sat beside me.

I introduced myself as the writer in the church and explained the reason for my visit—to gather information about their second son in order to write this book. Would they be willing to share their stories of his early years?

Memories flowed from the depths of the mother's heart. She had hidden them there, never expecting that she would one day share them with others. Her eyes brimmed with tears as she spoke.

A Mother Remembers

"Philip was born on September 27, 1974, the second of three sons. One night, he was sleeping soundly in his crib, when suddenly, I heard a piercing scream followed by the baby's frantic crying. My heart trembled with fear as I leapt from my chair and ran to his room. The crib was empty. Philip had climbed out of his crib and fallen. I picked him up and held him until his crying stopped.

"From that time on, he suffered from frequent convulsions. Even a low fever would bring one on. We took him to the doctor, but his condition did not improve. I knew something was wrong. In desperation, I prayed, 'Lord, please do not take him. I give this child to You. Please protect him, Lord' (see 1 Sam. 1:11).

"My vow, spoken from my heart, was a secret between me and the Lord. No one knew about it but Him. The good Lord heard my prayer. Philip began to grow and walk, and he rarely had convulsions anymore. I stopped giving him medicine.

"Philip was a frail child. His legs were weak, and he had difficulty walking. He would take three steps and fall. Yet I felt in my heart that this child was strong. His father recommended that we take him to an orthopedic surgeon, who said the bones in his legs and feet were not strong. The surgeon recommended that Philip wear corrective iron shoes to help his feet develop normally. They were heavy and uncomfortable, so Philip only wore them when we went out. The shoes made it very difficult for him to play, so every time I encouraged him to go outside and play, he refused. He always found an excuse not to go out in public because he was embarrassed by the iron shoes. He would say, 'Mom, I just want to stay home.'

"But after several months, the Lord strengthened his bones, and he never wore the shoes again."

"Even without the shoes, he wasn't having problems," said Hardi Mantofa, adjusting his glasses. The father continued to cut paper, occasionally adding to his wife's story. He seemed content to let her do most of the talking.

Lord, Change His Heart

"As the children grew, I promised the Lord that when Philip was three and one-half and his older brother Maxi was five, I would take them to church. Their father did not yet believe in the Lord Jesus. When I told him about my promise, he got angry.

"Because I didn't want to quarrel, I gave in and kept the boys home. But I took my burden to the Lord in prayer, always adding hopefully, 'Lord, change his heart.'

"Then, when Maxi was five and Philip was three and one-half, seemingly out of nowhere their father asked, 'Did you say you wanted to take them to church?'

"I immediately started taking both children to church and introduced them to Sunday school. Every day I told them stories about prominent characters in the Bible.

"Due to the limitations of Indonesia's educational system and the fact that few people outside of the country spoke the Indonesian language, it was common for wealthy parents to place their children in private schools or to send them abroad to study. That way, they not only got a good education, but they also became fluent in languages such as English and Mandarin Chinese, the official language of China.

"So when Philip was six and starting first grade, my husband and I agreed to send Maxi and Philip to their uncle and auntie for elementary school in Taiwan. That way Maxi, then seven, could be a friend for Philip.

"But he spent every day in Taiwan playing with his action figures for hours, and he didn't study. One day I arrived at their apartment while he was playing with the action figures. 'Philip, stop playing and go study,' I told him.

"He ignored me and kept playing. My patience gave out, and I took all the action figures and threw them out the window. He got angry. 'Mom, go home,' he said. 'You don't need to be here. Just go home to Indonesia.'

"The next day I packed my bags. I already planned the trip, but Philip didn't know about it. Philip sat on the apartment steps and watched me leave. I didn't know that after my departure, he sat there in the same spot every day and cried, asking Maxi, 'Why did Mama leave?'

"Maxi and Philip left Taiwan and returned to Indonesia, where they attended an elementary school and a Christian junior high school in Surabaya. Then Philip and his younger brother, John, went to school in Singapore for 1½ years and in 1990, when Philip was 16, we sent him and his brothers to Canada to continue their education."

Maxixe and Philip at Ho Bu Guo Xiao School, Taipei, Taiwan

The Fights Begin

"Maxi and Philip often got into fights during Sunday School. The scuffles continued as Philip got older. Right before he was to take a true-and-false test in school, Philip fought with a friend and broke his right hand, making it impossible for him to write. I reported the incident to his teacher, who let him take the exam by pointing to the correct answers with a nail. In Taiwan, when Philip was six, and Maxi seven, they started taking karate lessons. As Philip's skills increased, he picked fights more often.

"Maxi and Philip returned to Indonesia to finish elementary school and attend junior high school at St. Aloysius, in Kepanjen. But Philip's behavior did not improve. Every day he got into four or five fights. By his first year of junior high, he had nearly lost his life in violent encounters.

"His father and I knew Philip struggled with difficulties during his school-age years, but we were happy when he was finally able to overcome them. When he was delivered and baptized in Canada in 1992, he was no longer the same Philip as before. One reason his father accepted Jesus was because he saw the genuine change in Philip's life.

"It is the Lord who gives us every good thing. His father and I never take credit for the success of Philip's ministry. If the Lord has caused his ministry to excel, we know it is not because he is more outstanding than others, but because of God's grace.

"I believe my devoting Philip to the Lord when he was small, and my husband allowing the boys to go to church where they could hear the Word of God, was all part of the Lord's master plan."

My Life Principles

Honor your father and your mother, so that you may live long in the land the LORD your God is giving you (Exodus 20:12).

Honoring your father and mother is an unconditional requirement for a child. Of all the Lord's commands, this one seems the easiest. But it is only easy in theory. The reality of honoring our parents is not as simple as we might imagine.

To their children, parents are the representatives of God on this earth. It is proper that we honor and appreciate their decisions, as I believe that all parents want the best for their children's future.

My father didn't know the Lord when my mother dedicated me to Him. Because she was in tune with the Lord's plan, she desired not only for me to be healed, but to belong to the Lord— so she gave me to Him completely. The Lord honored her vow. Years later, I surrendered my life into Christ's hands.

When she prayed, "Lord, please do not take this child," she was a mother in despair. I do not know how many lost hopes my mother carried in her heart at that time. She might never have made that secret promise to the Lord if she thought I would survive. She feared that there was no hope for me, so she dedicated me to the Lord.

Irene, Philip, and Vanessa Mantofa

Today, when I face obstacles in the ministry, my parents respect my decisions. They have never regretted my decision to accept Christ's call and to take up the cross. Nonetheless, deep in their hearts, they both would have preferred for me to pursue business like their other two sons. But once they saw my total resolve, they let me go the way I had chosen. I am grateful for their blessing because I can honor them without sacrificing the glorious call of Christ on my life.

I cannot be sure of what will happen in the second half of my life, nor am I bold enough to predict success for the next ten years of my ministry. That's the Lord's job because He is the one who called me. I am certain of only one thing—I am only a child. No matter how much the Lord has used me, or how far He takes me, I know that in the eyes of my heavenly Father, Philip Mantofa is only a child. It's the same with my father and mother. In the Mantofa family, Philip is just a child who respects and honors his parents.

I have never regretted my mother's decision to surrender me to the Lord. In fact, I cannot imagine what it would be like if my

mother had not been bold enough to surrender her right as a parent to Him. Maybe I never would have met the Lord Jesus, my Savior. And if I had never met Him, my life would not be as meaningful and fulfilling as it is now.

My Father's Example

My father is a humble man who always extends his hand to help others and puts them before himself. When I come home, Papa always gets a drink and brings it to me. I learned how to serve from his example—handing someone a drink, a plate, or a chair before I help myself. Perhaps most people consider such an act so insignificant that anyone can do it. That is true. But unfortunately, most people don't think in terms of serving others. They are happier being served than being a servant. But my father is not like that. Though he is a quiet man, he always wants to help others. It is the example of his life that has made me comfortable making others my priority, even someone much younger than me. So I learned how to serve others at home. As the Bible says, "...*Honor one another above yourselves*" (Rom. 12:10).

The Lord has given me a wife, three children, and a precious ministry that enables me to give my best to Him. And it all started with my mama's prayer.

Chapter 1

Descent Into Darkness

SAID good-bye to Pastor Philip's parents and thanked them for opening their home and hearts to me and pulling back the curtain on their son's early years. Pastor Philip's older brother Maxi and younger brother John picked up the thread. The next season of the young man's life was a chilling encounter with evil that nearly took his life.

Maxi and John Remember

Before Philip met the Lord, his volatile emotions easily spiraled out of control, Maxi recalled. He would fly off the handle and hit people without provocation. Even a trivial problem could provoke him to rage.

He even chose to do evil to friends who crossed him, John said. When a friend accidentally ruined one of his cassettes, he repeatedly hit and kicked him in a fit of rage. Afterward, he kicked a Taiwanese student in the head until he passed out.

When Philip was six, karate lessons in Taiwan introduced him to the world of martial arts. As his strength and speed improved, his skills fueled his tendency to fight. When Maxi and Philip returned to Indonesia, the seeds of anger and belligerence that had taken root in Taiwan resurfaced. Every day Philip got into four to five fights. By his first year of junior high, he had been in several life-threatening confrontations.

By his first year of junior high, a fight outside of the school escalated dangerously after Philip beat up a senior. The senior's older brother showed up with a soldier wielding a knife. He screamed, waving his knife, "Where is Philip Mantofa? Come outside. I'll finish you off right now."

About 15 angry people were looking for his brother, Maxi said. Friends hid Philip to prevent his murder.

In another fight, his opponent throttled Philip and pinned him to the ground. His opponent's friends spotted a large rock right next to his head, and grabbed it to bash his head, but when Maxi intervened, Philip reversed the attack and was all over them. The next day, the four other boys went to school with their shoulders and hands bandaged because of broken bones. Philip and Maxi were called to the principal's office.

When Philip and John moved to Singapore to continue their studies, Philip picked fights with other students in the dormitory.

Even Toby, the dormitory dog, tasted his wrath. When Toby walked near a spill on the floor, he grabbed the dog and mopped the floor with its body. Once the floor was clean, he let Toby go. He thought it was funny to see the dog hurt.

Philip's most frightening fight erupted behind an apartment building in Singapore just hours before he and John returned home to Indonesia for vacation. In that skirmish, he fought off three opponents at the same time. John, accompanied by three other Indonesians, could only stand and watch without helping his brother.

"The fight was tense," John recalled. "In front of us stood a gang of Taiwanese, dozens of them. Our group was outnumbered. It wasn't a fair fight because it was three against one."

To John's astonishment, Philip singlehandedly defeated his three attackers and beat them black and blue.

"He easily beat up the first guy," John said. "Then, when his two buddies saw their friend sprawled on the ground, they attacked Philip from behind. Philip turned around and grabbed one of them. He beat him with one hand while his left hand seized the hair of the second. While he was busy with those two, a third attacker behind him struck him repeatedly. But strangely, he wasn't hurt."

Once again, Philip won. The brothers returned to their dorm, packed their things, and flew to Indonesia.

In 1990, when Maxi was 17, Philip, 16, and John, 12, the three brothers went to Vancouver, Canada to continue their studies. After a month, they started to attend Emmanuel Indonesian

(From left to right) John, Mr. Hardi, Philip, Maxixe Mantofa and
Mrs. Suzanna Lindawati, 1991

Christian Fellowship. Although they weren't yet born again, they often attended church with their friends.

During their first year in Vancouver, Maxi related another close call when Philip and his friends went to a Thai restaurant on Camby Street. While enjoying their food and karaoke, he spotted a Vietnamese gang leader, around 30 to 40 years old, sitting at another table.

The gang leader didn't like being observed, so he stared back at Philip belligerently. They watched each other angrily for several minutes, neither backing down. The gang leader took it as a challenge and became furious. He stood up and threw a glass at him. Fortunately, he missed, but that only fueled his anger.

As he approached Philip's table, intending to beat him up, Maxi jumped up and stood in front of Philip.

That only made things worse. Seeing tensions escalate, Maxi called 911. But before he was connected, the restaurant owner came over and separated them. The gang leader left the restaurant furious.

"We got home late that night to avoid being followed by the Vietnamese gang," Maxi recalled. "Although our house was only about an hour from the restaurant, we drove around in circles for three hours before going home."

My Life Principles

Let no one be found among you who sacrifices his son or daughter in the fire, who practices divination or sorcery, interprets omens, engages in witchcraft, or casts spells, or who is a medium or spiritist or who consults the dead. Anyone who does these things is detestable to the LORD, and because of these detestable practices the LORD your God will drive out those nations before you. You must be blameless before the LORD your God (Deuteronomy 18:10-13).

While I was in school in Singapore, I discovered a book on the occult in a local bookstore. I didn't understand how it happened, but that book opened the door to the occult in my life. At the time, I was just like other nominal Christians—I sinned, used curse words, and compromised here and there. I didn't hate God, but I didn't love Him, either.

I had begun to seek the Lord, but rejection, hatred, and bitterness were like bleeding wounds in my life. In Singapore, those bondages became worse. I was drawn to the occult because I was so disappointed in God. My perspective on the Lord was wrong, and heavy disappointments only made it worse. Sadly, some of those disappointments occurred just as I began to seek the Lord. I was too young and inexperienced in the Word and the Spirit to recognize the hand of the enemy trying to prevent me from drawing closer to Him. I also didn't know that the apostle Paul warned the Corinthians to make sure they forgave those who sinned against them "*lest Satan should take advantage of us; for we are not ignorant of his devices*" (2 Cor. 2:11 NKJV).

I lived in a boarding house with about 40 children from countries such as Thailand, Taiwan, Indonesia, and even from Singapore. I was in my first year of junior high school when the owner of the boarding house hired a tutor to teach us. He was a very smart man. Certain times were set aside for individual tutoring sessions.

This teacher was active in the church. He seemed very spiritual when he spoke. Every time he taught, he referred to the Lord. He even slipped spiritual insights into the math lessons. As a result, I started to get interested in seeking the Lord. I had never heard anyone speak about the Lord outside of church. As a matter of fact, the people I knew from church never referred to the Lord when they were outside the church walls. So I was drawn to this man whenever he spoke about the Lord. I don't know what made me so eager to know this Jesus he explained to us.

After he finished teaching, he did not always go home immediately. He would stay and trade stories with the children, stories about the Lord and other topics. I was happy. Once he spoke about contemporary music.

"Those contemporary songs are not good for you. Songs like that push us away from the Lord."

As soon as he finished his talk, I threatened everyone in the boarding house, "Whoever I meet who's still holding on to your contemporary music cassettes, I will beat you up."

The students were afraid of me, so they all gathered their cassette collections and threw them into large trash bags. I destroyed all those cassettes. It is obvious from the way that I handled that situation that I wanted to meet the Lord, but I didn't know how. I thought if I destroyed the cassettes by zeal and by force, I would find the Lord. I was wrong. The Lord didn't meet me after I did that.

Nevertheless, I was still enthusiastic to listen to this teacher. Every time he taught, I listened quietly, taking it all in. My heart was so thirsty for the Lord—until the teacher discovered my interest in his spiritual stories. He took advantage of my hunger for the Lord by inflicting a new wound in my heart.

Apparently, this teacher was attracted to young boys. One by one, he deceived every young boy he could, including me. He was a sick man who used the guise of religion to get what he wanted. Once when I was alone in a room, he told me to take my clothes off. Then he groped me. All I could do was stand still like a statue from shock. I didn't cry out for help, but I didn't run away, either. I was accomplished at karate and could have incapacitated him with a single blow. But I was hesitant. I thought he was a pastor. How could I kick a pastor? All those spiritual stories paralyzed me. I was confused. When it crossed my mind to hit him, I thought, *Maybe this is what God told him to do.* I did not yet understand anything about the Lord.

That incident severely disappointed and discouraged me, adding to a long list of causes for bitterness and rejection that were already smoldering inside me. I got angry at the Lord. I questioned His existence because of the bitter experiences in my life.

"Wasn't I seeking You, Lord?" I cried out. "Why did You mislead me? Why didn't You do something? Why did You allow that to happen?"

Later, I realized that what that teacher had done was wrong. But at that time, disappointment oppressed me and my spirit became more and more empty. My mama always included Bible verses in her letters, but they had no effect. Going to church couldn't fill my spiritual emptiness, either. I attended once in a while, but the church was not alive. They did not believe in the works of the Holy Spirit. After that, no one helped me find a way to escape my bitterness and disappointment, so I tried to find a way out myself. I thought I had found the answer in the book on the occult.

A Turn Down the Wrong Road

I began to study meditation and other teachings in that book. On Saturdays, when everyone else took the day off, I stayed in my room and meditated. I turned out the lights and closed the door. My room didn't have a window, so my room was private and I was free to practice my meditation. Sitting in front of the mirror, I would gaze into my own eyes until I went into a trance. The book taught me that I could find a power within myself, to control the universe and my surroundings, as well as my emotions and myself through meditation. These seemed like good and positive ideas, but I had to search for it by emptying my thoughts and myself through meditation. Many tenets and teachings of Eastern religions were combined in this book and many others like it that I read. I practiced everything these books taught.

I thought I needed that power because I had many enemies. It was actually true that I needed extra strength. It was normal for five to ten people to gang up on me on a daily basis. That drove me even more deeply into practicing meditation, and I often went into trances. At one point, I experienced an astral body—when my spirit took flight and I could see my body from a distance. I now know by God's Word and His truth that it was a sham, the trickery of the devil, *"the working of Satan, with all power, signs, and lying wonders"* (2 Thess. 2:9 NKJV).

Without my awareness, those times of emptying myself exposed my heart to be inhabited by many devils (see Matt. 12:43-45a). But that wasn't all. In the process, I also emptied myself of all my desires, reason, and human wisdom. It was like opening wide the door into my life. Once that door was opened, evil spirits entered. My life began to spiral out of control. But I didn't realize it at first.

As I began practicing the occult teachings in those books, I felt a pseudo satisfaction, as though I had obtained a higher level of spirituality. But unsettling changes occurred at the same time. When Toby, the boarding house dog, saw me, he would run in fear as if he had seen a ghost. He would yelp suddenly and hide under the bed. That dog did not want to be anywhere near me. I also started losing friends because of my strange behavior.

When I got angry, I had less self-control, and in a flash, my conscious thought life would disappear. When I regained awareness, I would see five to ten people collapsed on the floor, beaten black and blue. I had no idea what had happened until someone asked me, "Why did you beat up those people?"

I didn't know why, and I certainly did not know I was possessed. Is it possible for a person who is possessed to know he's possessed? I first became aware of it when I started to lose my memory. It happened more frequently, especially during my fights in Singapore. I became invincible. If I was hit, I did not feel pain. The book promised I would be victorious by following its steps, and it seemed to be true. Every time I fought, I won. I never lost, no matter how large my opponent was or whether he had a black belt in one of the martial arts. I didn't care. I was once hit repeatedly with a baseball bat, but there was no damage to my body at all, not even a mark. I didn't feel even the slightest pain. When I regained awareness of my surroundings, I saw all my opponents scattered on the floor. I could control my anger up to a point. But when hatred overcame my heart, I became possessed (see Mark 5:1-7).

Since I had been young, my mother had taught me about Christianity and God's Word. But during that time, I became a hater of God and His Word. I also hated the Bible and church praise and worship songs. I had not been like that before, but I couldn't fight it. I was getting further and further away from God.

> *Don't you know that when you offer yourselves to someone to obey him as slaves, you are slaves to the one whom you obey—whether you are slaves to sin, which leads to death, or to obedience, which leads to righteousness?... What benefit did you reap at that time from the things you are now ashamed of ? Those things result in death!* (Romans 6:16,21)

Chapter 2

I Saw Jesus

ONE afternoon I had a conversation with Pastor Philip in his office while he was sitting on the sofa eating lunch.

"Pastor Philip, why do you give so many opportunities to people who don't deserve it? You give them another chance, yet they still don't change. Why? What do you see in them?"

He smiled.

"Because the Lord did that for me, Sianne. I didn't deserve grace, but He gave it to me anyway—not just once, but every time. So I give the same grace I received from the Lord to others."

Questions arose in my mind, but I couldn't bring myself to ask them. He stopped eating and leaned back on the sofa.

"I do it even when I don't have a good reason because I'm convinced that when they find their calling, they'll do the same."

All day his words haunted me. As I reflected on what Pastor Philip was like before he met the Lord, I wanted to know more about how God's grace delivered him from his shackles and transformed his life. Perhaps telling his story would enable others to receive grace, and then let it flow through them to others. I asked Maxi to tell me about his brother's transformation in Canada.

A Frightening Spiritual Encounter

"During his high school years in Canada, Philip was very sensitive and easily depressed," Maxi said. "He often seemed as if he had no hope, though I didn't understand why. Though it took me awhile to realize the intensity of the struggle going on in his life, I began to get the picture one night in 1991. That was the first time I saw him seek God sincerely.

"I was downstairs watching television and Philip was sleeping on the second floor. I went upstairs to sleep, but as I lay down, Philip burst into the room. He was having difficulty breathing and his face was ashen. 'Brother, I was attacked by satan,' he said.

"I was not very spiritual back then, so fear surfaced in my heart. 'What do you mean? How did he attack you?'

"Philip said, 'I felt like sleeping on the floor, so I put my pillow on the carpet and lay down. Suddenly, I felt like someone was wringing my neck, and I couldn't open my mouth to call for help.

I heard a sound like the stomping of soldiers' iron boots—stomp, stomp, stomp. The marching was unbearably loud, right next to my ear. I tried to call out for you, but my tongue was struck dumb. I couldn't move or even stand up. As I tried to call you, I heard a whisper in my ear: "You're pretty brave when your older brother is around. But when you're alone, you're not so brave."'

"Philip had been attending church perfunctorily, so at least he'd been exposed to God's Word. At that moment, he remembered that our pastor, Sonny Mandagie, said there was power in the name of Jesus (see Eph. 1:21). So Philip called on the name on the Lord.

"'In the name of Jesus, in the name of Jesus, in the name of Jesus,' he said silently, in his heart. After that, he could raise his neck and head. He heard the boots slowly march away. The stomping grew more distant and finally disappeared.

"When John got home, Philip told him the story. The three of us were afraid to sleep alone that night, so we all slept together in John's room."

Angels Around Us

"Although we were together, fear overshadowed us. No one could help us that night. As the older brother, whether I wanted to or not, I knew that I had to take responsibility for my two younger brothers. So I prayed and asked for God's forgiveness. Then I requested His protection.

John, Philip, and Maxixe, Canada

"When I finished praying, the Lord gave me a vision: I was flying above our house and could clearly see the roof below. As I looked down, I saw many beautiful winged creatures wearing robes of white, circling the roof of our home. I was filled with awe and great peace, and I knew that the Lord had answered my prayer. So I told my younger brothers, 'Be calm. I see many angels circling over our home. We can sleep peacefully tonight.' That night I felt God's peace. Fear no longer controlled my heart.

"Of the three of us, John was the most spiritual. When we first moved to Canada, John was the most active in spiritual matters. He played guitar, joined a Bible study, and got involved in many church activities. So he was actually the "oldest" in that room spiritually speaking. Nevertheless, God honored my prayers as the older brother. That night we prayed together. Afterward, we could all sleep."

The Gift of Discernment

"Although Philip did not yet know the Lord, God began to use his sensitivity in a positive way—with spiritual discernment (see 1 Cor. 4:10). On a visit to Canada, Mama and Papa gave us three stackable porcelain elephants—large, medium, and small. Mama fondly told us the elephants were symbolic of us three boys. We put them near the television. One afternoon when I came home, the elephants were missing. I asked Philip where they were.

"'I threw them away,' he answered. 'I saw a spirit leaving those elephants.' The hairs on the nape of my neck stood up. That was the second time Philip had seen a manifestation of satan in our house.

"A third supernatural occurrence took place when Philip, John, Mama, and I were fixing up the basement so that Philip and I could move in there and share the spacious room. At one point, I left the room. When I returned, Philip told me he had heard the voice of a woman singing in Cantonese, the language of Hong Kong. No one was in the room but him. He said he was learning to pray when he heard the voice.

"Another time, when I returned from a trip, I couldn't find my favorite cassettes. I asked Philip if he had seen them. 'I threw them away,' he said. 'Some speakers at a church seminar said that if you play them backwards, you'll hear the words of satan.'"

Spiritual Awakening

"I began to understand that Philip would one day be called and used by the Lord, although at that time, he still was not right with God. He wanted to learn to submit to the Lord, so he began to pray, read the Bible, and obey.

"I could no longer be the older brother who gave him spiritual advice. Sometimes when evil spirits troubled him, I could not invite him to pray. Occasionally I said the wrong things, and he became angrier. I was rebuking not satan, but Philip. I did not know what to do. I became more and more confused.

"As Philip went through a process of being changed by the Lord, he still struggled with outbursts of rage. He took out his anger on anyone or anything in his path. The walls in Canada were gypsum, and in our home, the wall by the stairwell to the second floor has three holes gouged by Philip's fists. I wasn't brave enough to call a repairman, so I repaired them myself as best I could.

"Philip wasn't the only one going through spiritual warfare. During the same time, satan was harassing many friends from our church. God was permitting satan to test those He planned to use (see Job 1:8-12; 2:3-7; Luke 4:1).

"Philip didn't change overnight. It was a process that took time, as repentance and the desire to know God worked in his heart. But once he received deliverance, he repented and a desire was birthed in him to serve the Lord."

A New Creation

> *Therefore, if anyone is in Christ, he is a new creation; the old has gone, the new has come!* (2 Corinthians 5:17)

"From the day that Philip gave his whole heart to the Lord, he did not live any longer like the Philip we knew. He diligently prayed and read his Bible. If he was somewhere he couldn't pray, he took his guitar, went to the restroom, closed the stall door, and sat and praised the Lord there. That became his private place for worship, and that's where he received the baptism of the Holy Spirit—while he was singing to the Lord."

My Life Principles

> *Therefore, I tell you, her many sins have been forgiven-- for she loved much. But he who has been forgiven little loves little."* (Luke 7:47).

Before I met the Lord, I habitually committed small sins, which slowly matured and produced death (see Rom. 6:16). Actually, I was already close to death. As a result, I truly appreciate my salvation. My friends in Vancouver used to say, "We're all sinners. But there are some among us who feel the most sinful." I am one of those. That is why the story of Mary of Bethany, the sinner woman who loved Jesus, is so close to my heart (see Luke 7:36-59).

Who do you think loves Jesus more— those who are forgiven much or those who are forgiven little? Both are sinners, but some feel their sin is greater. When the Lord saves people like these, they often love Him more than others do. That's not because the Lord loves them more, but because they feel so unworthy to receive His love.

I still include myself among them. Although the past has lost its sting because of His redemption, I cannot forget it. And so I give thanks every day. I am in the same class as that prostitute. She sinned much and felt unworthy, but she loved the Lord more than those around her because she had been forgiven of more.

If someone owes you $50,000 and someone else owes you $50 million, when you forgive both debtors, who will love you more? Of course, the one who owes more. I owed $50 million, but Jesus Christ released me from all my debts of sin, and paid the price on the cross. So I know how unworthy I am. Yet...

> *The Lord is merciful and gracious, slow to anger, and abounding in mercy. He will not always strive with us, nor will He keep His anger forever. He has not dealt with us according to our sins, nor punished us according to our iniquities. For as the heavens are high above the earth, so great is His mercy toward those who fear Him; as far as the east is from the west, so far has He removed our transgressions from us. As a father pities his children, so the Lord pities those who fear Him* (Psalm 103:8-13 NKJV).

When I moved to Canada, my bondages got worse. As a result of studying the occult, I got involved in pornography and other sins. I had thought that by leaving Singapore, I could leave the events there behind and they would be forgotten. I was wrong. Those traumas could not be erased from my memory. Three hours before I left Singapore I was fighting with some Taiwanese.

John, Philip, and Maxixe, Canada

Even though I was winning at fights, they were beginning to traumatize me. I felt like a troublemaker. My life had started out ugly and it was ending ugly. I began to have doubts. I no longer felt invincible.

Nevertheless, in Vancouver I began to see the two sides of the spiritual realm. The first side of spirituality I experienced was darkness, though at the time, I didn't discern that darkness. On the other hand, I also saw the spiritual side of God's children. They were so enthusiastic that, at first, I thought they were fanatics. They praised the Lord, clapped their hands, leapt, and witnessed to others outside of the church. It amazed me. They often said they heard God's voice. That was something new for me.

Both sides attracted my attention. I didn't want to let go of my darkness, but I was also attracted to the other side. I vacillated between the two for a while. But, little by little, my carnality and anger resurfaced. I began to resent the fact that John, my younger brother, was growing in the Lord. I began to feel there was something wrong with me. I sensed an evil presence dwelling inside me.

Every time Maxi talked about the Lord, it aggravated me and stirred up the evil spirits. When that aggravation overcame my heart, I would suddenly lose all awareness of myself and my surroundings. When that happened, I was possessed. When I fought my family, I became powerful. Maxi was tall, but if I barely touched him, he was thrown aside. No one was strong enough to hold me down. Yet I was not conscious when these things happened.

Many of my memories from that period have been lost. Before I repented in Canada, perhaps 25 percent of my life was lived under demonic possession. If I was angry, my eyes would turn red. My strength was abnormal when I was angry. I became fierce. I also became suicidal. Once, in a rage, I drank the alcohol on the shelf at home until I was drunk. Then I drove really fast. Gradually, friends realized something was wrong with me.

I began to suspect it as well. I became a thief for the first time. I stole something from a department store. The security staff was surprised to find a wad of money in my pocket. "Why do you steal when you have a lot of money and credit cards?" they asked.

I didn't know. But before I was caught, a voice instructed me, "Take that thing. Steal it."

I was arrested, taken to the police station, and interrogated. But the police never knew that there were evil spirits living in me with free reign to control me. Bitterness was the strong man—an open door that had introduced me to the world of darkness.

I felt increasingly empty and oppressed by the demons. They constantly interfered with my life. The power of darkness was so real that I was threatened when I thought about getting more involved in church. Every day I became more drawn to Pastor Sonny's church, Emmanuel Indonesian Christian Fellowship.

One evening, some older brothers and sisters in the Lord came to my house for a prayer meeting. As we prayed together, I burst out, "May I learn how to pray?"

They answered, "Yes, of course." But the look in their eyes seemed to say, "Be careful. Philip is not normal."

My prayer was brief, "Lord Jesus, please bless 'A' and 'B,' in Jesus' name. Amen."

After we finished praying together, I fell asleep on the floor. Suddenly I heard the buzz of a bee. Bzzz…bzzzz… My body felt as if someone was strangling and forcefully constraining me. It was as if a bee had entered my feet. Something was oppressing me so heavily that it was difficult to move. I realized it was an evil spirit. That was the first time I experienced the manifestation of an evil spirit directly. Up to that moment, the demons had always protected me. But as soon as I used the name of Jesus to pray for someone, they turned against me.

I was not yet born again, but I wanted to learn how to pray for others, beginning with the friends who were an example to me. That small gathering in my home where I learned to join in prayer was a turning point. Apparently, the evil spirits were mad at me.

The demons ramped up the pressure. From the first day that they tried to silence me so I couldn't pray, every time I closed my eyes to pray, it felt as if someone let their fist fly at me. Then I heard the sound of feet—stomp, stomp, stomp—like soldiers marching in unison. The sound was very clear, directly in front of me, close to my face. Every day, two to three times a day, devils visited my room and I heard terrifying voices.

Every time the evil spirits tried to strangle me, I tried to scream for help, but could not. I tried to stand up, but could not. I gasped for breath. It was difficult to breathe because their choke-hold was so strong. It seemed they wanted to kill me. Although I was awake when these events occurred, I didn't want to tell anyone because I was afraid no one would believe me. When I told one person about it, he just laughed at me. So I kept those terrifying stories to myself.

An evil spirit once tried to strangle me when I was in a biology class. I couldn't do anything because there were a lot of people around me, so I remained silent. The others were not paying attention to me, although I literally felt like I was being strangled to death.

Once I tried to stand up to ask for help when suddenly, the keys of my computer keyboard started moving as if someone was walking on them. My room was filled with evil spirits. Then I remembered one of my pastor's sermons, which taught us that the name of Jesus has power and authority. So I immediately put that into practice.

When I tried to call out the name of Jesus, something tried to strangle me. But I also felt another power helping me. I did not know if it was an angel or the Holy Spirit, but finally, with great difficulty I called out the name of Jesus. Immediately, all the harassing spirits stopped what they were doing and vanished. There were no more clicking sounds from the computer keyboard. Silence. Immediately I stood up and ran out of my room.

Aside from those incidents, my life seemed normal. My grades were good. So I understood why no one realized something serious was happening in my life. On the rare occasions when I tried to reach out to others, they didn't understand. My friends attributed my behavior to stupidity. They didn't understand that I wasn't conscious at certain times because I was under another power. I am convinced that even those at my church did not understand. Every time I tried to explain these things to a friend at church, he said, "Just take some medicine. Get some rest. Maybe you have a little flu." So I didn't want to talk about what I was going through, because no one took me seriously.

Brush With Death

One day, alone in the basement, my hatred toward the Lord and myself overwhelmed me. I was bitterly disappointed in my family, friends, and church. My days seemed so dark. Angrily and impudently, I cursed, blasphemed, even threatened Him and challenged Him to a fight. I threw the Bible on the floor, stepped on it, and spit on it. Then I said, "I am better off in hell than meeting the Lord."

As soon as I said that, my chest thundered as if from an overdose of a powerful stimulant. My heart was beating too fast, and I collapsed like someone slain in the spirit, only harder. It was like being slugged. Maybe an angel struck me.

When I collapsed on the floor, my heart was beating frantically. What happened next will always be for me what has made it impossible for me not to love the Lord. My breathing became tight, though normally my heart was strong. I knew I was dying. Then suddenly, I felt the presence of the Lord.

I heard a voice speak to my heart and my ears. He said, "I love you."

The Battle for My Soul

> So Jacob was left alone, and a man wrestled with him till daybreak (Genesis 32:24).

Truly amazing. But I still hadn't learned my lesson. When I heard the Lord say He loved me, my heartbeat became stable again. But I stood up again, and I blasphemed for the second time. I was thrown to the floor again, and my heart beat frantically—this time even harder than the first.

His presence returned. I was alone in that room with Jesus. When His presence came down, I cried like a baby. I wept because of His voice that said, "I love you." There on the floor, I screamed.

"Why do You love me? I don't love You. Kill me now. Do it now while I hate You. Punish me now."

Sobbing aloud, with my eyes swollen, I rejected God's love.

For the third time, I stood up and blasphemed. This time my breath was really constricted. I was unable to breathe several times. For the third time, I was thrown down onto the floor and struck it with a loud thud. Boom! Hearing it, John, who had arrived home, came down from the second floor. My heart was beating hard, and I was gasping for breath like a fish out of water. I knew, even though I could not see it, that an angel stood before me and wanted to strike me. I knew that if he hit me even once, I would die.

For a moment, terror overwhelmed me. Yet, despite all this, my heart was too hard to repent. I was too haughty to ask for help from the Lord Jesus. So what did He do? His presence came down and covered me. And when His presence came down, I heard a voice say to my heart, very clearly, as if weeping, "I love you."

My heartbeat returned to normal and I could breathe again. Then John came in.

"What is it, bro? What's going on?"

I cursed at him, and he left. Then I made a decision.

"OK. You don't want to kill me. Then I'll kill myself."

Amazing Grace

Three times I planned to kill myself. But strangely, for some reason, I failed every time. The first and second attempt failed because I thought about my family. If I committed suicide, how would they handle it? On the third attempt, I resolved not to think of my parents again. I was determined not to fail. I wanted to be free once and for all from the constant harassment of the evil spirits.

This time I would make sure nothing would cause me to fail. My brothers were not at home. I locked the house and went into my bedroom. I felt hopeless. Even my friends said I was hopeless. When one friend, Robert T., prayed for me, he shook his head, and said, "Only the Lord can make him turn around. Only He can save him. No one else can help him. He's too stubborn." When I was saved, he was the person who was most amazed.

I had already decided that it was better to enter hell than to meet the Lord. I was disappointed in my family, my friends, and my church. Why was I close to evil spirits? Because the only place I could express my true feelings was when I meditated. I was deceived, for I had come to believe that the Lord was evil. In my eyes, the heavenly Father carried a whip in His hand, like a father who liked to punish and constantly pointed out my mistakes. But it was the devil who had planted those lies in my mind. I had swallowed his lies whole.

I was also under a spirit of condemnation. I thought Jesus' sacrifice on the cross was for everyone except for the worst sinners, like me. I thought I was the exception, that the Lord Jesus died only for good people. I didn't want to go to Heaven. I believed I'd be better off going to hell with the devil. At least he resembled me and understood my feelings The devil had reversed the truth. And when I remembered the words of my Christian friend, who said I was hopeless, I wanted to kill myself even more.

Other friends prayed for me. One Christian brother suspected there were evil spirits in my life. When he prayed for me, that same night he was visited by an evil spirit, who oppressed and tried to strangle him. My younger brother was once beaten by demons until his stomach hurt. When these things happened, they reinforced my feelings that I was forsaken by God and cursed. I felt too dirty. I thought it was impossible for me to be saved.

I closed the door and locked it. I took a sharp object and prepared to cut my artery. Suddenly the telephone rang. I had forgotten to yank out the cord. It was Ina, my pastor's wife.

I did not commit suicide. That phone call saved me. It was as if the Lord wanted to warn me: "Stop messing around. Hell is a very unpleasant place."

I finally understood that the evil spirits did not give me the things of this world free of charge, but that they also had a contract out for my soul. *"The wages of sin is death…"* (Rom. 6:23). I almost paid that penalty. But God miraculously showed His grace to me when I was in a precarious place, in a free fall to hell. I know that I am just a piece of trash, like a cigarette butt plucked from a burning fire. I am purely a product of grace.

I Saw Jesus

Two weeks later I went to church. I was not new to church services and God's Word about receiving Jesus indicated there would be an altar call in a moment. I got ready to leave. Soon the praises rose, and the pastor made an invitation for those who wanted to receive Christ. The congregation stood and sang. Again I heard the pastor invite those who had not yet received Christ to come forward. I stood up and started moving toward the exit. My hand was reaching for the doorknob when I heard a man's voice in my ear. It was an audible voice, firm and loud, not a voice from within my heart.

"Philip. If you are not saved today, you will be lost forever."

I was surprised and turned my head to the left and the right. I wanted to know who had spoken so loudly to me. But no one was standing near me, and all eyes were closed. I was alone. I was enveloped by fear and not brave enough to leave the church. Then I realized that I had heard God's voice. It was the same voice I had heard in the basement of my house, that gentle voice that said, "I love you."

Immediately I ran to the front and lifted up my hands. I cried like a small child. I didn't care anymore what the people around me thought. I saw the congregation, the pastor, and the song leader singing one song over and over. But that lasted only a moment. Not long after that, I saw a very bright light encompassing the room from the front all the way to those sitting in the very back.

That light was so bright that it erased even the shadows of the people near me. The entire space became very bright. Not long after that, I couldn't see anyone else. Even the sound of the praises became softer and after a while was lost. Total silence. Sometimes I blinked my eyes to be certain I was still there among them. But I could not see anything except that light. I could not hear any voices except the voice of the Lord.

I did not yet know about the experience of the apostle Paul, who had seen a bright light (see Acts 22:6). My friends did not see the light. All they heard were the words coming from my mouth (see Acts 22:9). They didn't realize that I met the Lord.

God's intervention through that light saved my life. But I did not fall or faint. At the end of the service I was still standing. I was completely conscious, only covered by the power of the Lord Jesus. Suddenly, from behind that light came an audible voice, very clear. I heard His voice very close to me, but I could not see His face. Perhaps if I had seen His face, I would have died.

Very clearly, He said to me in English, "I am Jesus, and I love you."

Spontaneously, I cried like a small child. When I heard the words, "I am Jesus, and I love you," it was as if my entire body was splashed with clean and refreshing cold water. All my filthiness, from my head to my toes, was washed clean. All my chains, from top to bottom, were broken. With only that one sentence from Him, I felt all those shackles removed from me. I cried again like a child, then asked, "Why?"

The Lord did not answer. I shouted to Him, "Lord, let me die for You. I am not worthy."

He responded with an unfathomable answer: "No. Live for Me instead."

That encounter seemed to be over quickly, but the congregation actually waited a long time for me. Everyone else had returned to their seats. When I looked around, I was suddenly aware that I was alone up front. That day He touched me and I was changed. For the first time, I accepted the love of the Lord, and I fell in love with Him. I finally surrendered.

A New Walk

Afterward, the Lord freed me from the evil spirits over a period of 40 days, without human assistance. At the end of that time, I received human help. Pastor Sonny cast out the last evil spirit from within me.

The first evil spirit that Jesus sovereignly cast out was the spirit of martial arts. Apparently, my former oath of karate-ka had caused that spirit to enter my body. The last to leave was the spirit of bitterness. That was the one Pastor Sonny cast out.

During those 40 days of deliverance by the Lord, I was sitting at home, praying and reading the Bible, when suddenly my hands began to shake. Moved by the Holy Spirit, I placed my hand on my chest. At the same moment, I felt as if something was moving inside my body. When I placed my hand on my stomach, it moved up. Then the Holy Spirit gave me wisdom and

I placed my hand on my neck. Again, whatever was moving was bound. Suddenly I vomited. In the vomit was a lot of blood.

Afterward I gradually experienced more deliverance. One day, I walked into the living room and suddenly collapsed. My body felt weak as an evil spirit left. The Lord told me that He would not cast out all the spirits at the same time. I remembered reading about God's promise to the nation of Israel concerning the foreign nations that surrounded them. The Lord said He would not drive away the Canaanites, the Hittites, and the Amorites all at once, because if all of them were expelled at the same time, the wild animals would increase and prey upon them (see Deut. 7:22). The Lord spoke to me during those days:

"I will not cast out everything at once because there are so many. I will cast them all out over a period of 40 days. While casting them out, I will cause your spirit to grow. Ever since you were small, your spirit has been controlled by evil spirits. Therefore, your spirit was dead and didn't grow. I will cause it to grow so that later, when they are all out, you will not die."

Slowly I opened up to the ministry of the Holy Spirit. During those 40 days I experienced strange things. Once, I woke up feeling weak and lying on the floor, as the spirits exited my body. Things like that happened for 40 days. Every day the spirits left in various ways.

The last one left at a prayer meeting one morning in Canada. The Lord had told me to go there, but as soon as I woke up, the evil spirit oppressed me so much that I become anxious and didn't want to leave. Two conflicting thoughts raged in my

Philip and Vanessa (This is the place where Phillip saw Jesus.)

heart. I wanted to go, but the evil spirit inside me, the spirit of bitterness, fought to maintain his stronghold.

The night before, all my bitterness had suddenly returned. Memories of my bitter disappointment in Singapore resurged, transporting me back to my dark past. The memories were so vividly oppressive that I wanted to kill that teacher. I decided not to go to the prayer meeting. I went to bed at 4 A.M. so that I wouldn't wake up early enough the next day. But at exactly 7 A.M. I woke up and sat up, refreshed. I said with my mouth, "I don't want to go. I don't want to go." But I went to the bathroom, brushed my teeth, got my car keys, and turned on the engine. Although my mouth and heart continued to repeat, "I don't want to go," the Holy Spirit propelled me to church.

I arrived at the church and entered the room where the prayer meeting would be held. There were less than ten people present. One was a man in his 50s we called "Uncle John." He was holding a guitar. As I sat down, he sang an old, popular song:

> *The peace He has given is so great*
> *Peace that makes my heart delight*
> *God is with me along my way*
> *I surrender all to Him, Lord Jesus*

As he sang, my body began to sink to the floor. The people around me knew that I was about to experience deliverance. My thoughts were divided—40 percent were possessed and 60 percent were weakening. All my bitterness came to the surface. Lili, my spiritual older sister, was sitting next to me and saw the change. When my face furrowed, she began to stroke my head. While she stroked, I felt the Lord's love again. Previously, all my thoughts had been controlled by that demon. That day, I said to the devil: "Hey, satan, starting today I want no part of you. Jesus loves me very much. I do not want you!"

That's the last thing I remember. The rest I heard from other people's stories. They told me I threw a chair. Suddenly a manifestation of demon spirits occurred. I couldn't see. It was chaos. Lili stepped aside and Pastor Sonny moved quickly to my side. He grabbed my head and neck, and with a loud shout cried, "Unclean spirit, I command you to go, in Jesus' name!"

Baptized at Salmon Arm Lake, September 7, 1992

"Unclean spirit" were the last words I heard before I lost consciousness. My friends told me I collapsed to the ground while holding onto Pastor Sonny's legs. My legs were kicking like people do in tae kwon do. After Pastor Sonny cast the evil spirit out of my body, I threw up. The spirit of bitterness left completely. When I regained consciousness, I was embracing Pastor Sonny's knees and crying and whispering, "Father, yes, Father." I felt the love of the Father through Pastor Sonny.

Chapter 3

Heaven Called My Name

IN 2004, when Pastor Philip attended his grandmother's funeral service in Surabaya, he stood before hundreds of unbelievers and boldly proclaimed God's call on his life. Although he knew his listeners held pastors in low esteem, he announced his pastoral office for a reason. Indonesia is a predominantly Muslim country, and many of his relatives were hostile to Christianity and distrustful of pastors. But he was prepared to risk being ridiculed or rejected.

"My name is Philip Mantofa. I am my grandmother's only grandchild who is a pastor."

Then he cast the net and preached to the crowd as they laughed, talked, and ate watermelon seeds and peanuts. At first, only a few listened to his sermon. Most ignored him. But he did not change his preaching style. As enthusiastic and bold as always, he proclaimed God's beautiful calling on his life.

Some people standing by me made comments like, "Why is Philip talking so loudly? His voice is getting hoarse." Another asked, "Is this a revival service?"

"It was God's calling," Philip continued.

Pastor Philip's brother, Maxi, understood the bias that existed in their family and hometown, and he refuted their preconceived notions, one by one.

"Philip did not become a pastor because he couldn't find a steady job or a promising career," Maxi told me. "It wasn't because he was stupid, either. Philip was a top student, number one in his class. And he didn't become a pastor because he was poor and had no other options. Our family is well-to-do.

"During his ministerial internship in Ungaran in 1994, he lived without many of the comforts he was used to," Maxi continued. "Although Philip was used to fancy cars, in Ungaran, a small town in Central Java, he walked or took public transportation without complaining.

"If the Lord had not called him, he never could have survived," Maxi observed. "When he came home from Ungaran, he showed us a slideshow of his living quarters. I was disgusted. If he hadn't been called by God, he would never have agreed to live there."

When Philip's mother saw the slides of the wet, filthy bathroom floor, she remarked that Philip was very fastidious and didn't like going into bathrooms with wet floors. If he had to, he would stand on his tiptoes.

Although his family was wealthy, when Pastor Philip traveled to Ungaran, he intentionally carried exact change. He also insisted that his mother not send him any money. He wanted to learn responsibility for the Lord's call on his life and trust in Him to provide without burdening his family.

Ungaran 1994

"Last year, our papa wanted to buy him a Mercedes for his birthday," Maxi said. "Philip really liked fancy cars, but when Papa mentioned it to him, he turned down the offer. He said that since many of his spiritual children had to walk or take public transportation, how could he as their spiritual father drive a Mercedes?

"That must not have been easy, Sianne," Maxi said. "I'm not certain that I'd be willing to live like that. When Philip told about his life in Ungaran, how he had to bathe and brush his teeth in water full of mosquito larva, in my heart I thought, *Now you know the consequences of becoming a pastor.*"

Mrs. Samuel Handoko, his pastor's wife at Maranatha Church, in Ungaran, echoed Maxi's observations. "In Ungaran he did not want to be treated as special," she said. "He never complained

Pastor Philip's house and its interior in Vancouver, Canada.

because the meals were not nutritious or what he was used to. He seldom ate out, either. He ate whatever I prepared," she said softly. "Once he wanted to buy bread worth less than two cents in U.S. currency, but his money was limited," she said. That was the first time he had to think twice before buying bread.

When he came down with a high fever, he was so sick he couldn't stand up. All he could do was to lay down every day in his room, where the roof had sprung several leaks. Senior Pastor Samuel Handoko and his wife offered to take him to a doctor several times, but he refused. Finally, when Irene, his fiancée (now his wife) in Surabaya, heard he was sick, she traveled to Ungaran to look in on him and insisted that he see a doctor.

"We had a difficult time," Mrs. Sam said. "In our house there were leaks everywhere, including Philip's room. The place we now use as

Bathroom and toilet in Ungaran, 1994

an office was a partitioned warehouse. That's where he slept. He was polite and not fussy. He adapted easily and did not complain.

"Usually it's difficult for the son of wealthy parents to accept these kinds of conditions. But Philip was different. He did not grumble; although almost every day I gave him only vegetables. I wanted to give him meat more often, but I couldn't afford it."

The Pastoral Calling

> *I came to you in weakness and fear, and with much trembling* (1 Corinthians 2:3).

I understood Pastor Philip because I am a pastor's daughter. Of all nine siblings, not one of us wanted to be a pastor. We were all involved in volunteer ministries at church. But to become a pastor—the only one who would raise their hand is me. And that is because I am the child of a vow.

Not many people I knew dreamed of becoming a pastor. There were so many other choices in this world—why a pastor? I wondered how many students at Bible or theological schools around the world had truly been called by God. How many came out of a pure motivation to serve Him and not for other reasons?

I knew that unless someone is called by the Lord and committed to His call, the pressures would be impossible to bear. Entering the Lord's harvest field means being prepared to face anything, and it requires picking up your cross to follow Jesus. Pastor Philip knew that God's call to the ministry would mean crucifying the flesh (see Luke 4:27; Gal. 5:24). Indeed, he faced many challenges.

He tried to understand others, whether they understood him or not. He always gave others opportunities and the benefit of the doubt, whether they reciprocated or not. He often cried in his closet, presenting his case before the Lord. No one knew what he suffered except him and the Lord.

He disciplined himself so that his weaknesses would not impact his spiritual children. He once asked a pastor, "If I am weak, how can I strengthen the people I lead? Who will my spiritual children run to? Many people pressure me and say I am overly confident. But I have weaknesses and I too get discouraged. However, I don't allow those weaknesses to overpower me. I run to the Lord, who refreshes my heart. That way I am strong enough to bear the pressures and my own weaknesses. The only one I allow to know when I am weak is the Lord, not my spiritual children."

As a pastor's daughter, I realized that being a leader is not easy, especially for a public figure like Pastor Philip. One wrong word could impact the lives of many others. As his ministry expanded, he had to grapple not only with want and opposition, but also with success.

"Sianne, I am very afraid the Lord is jealous of me because people often look to me instead of to the Lord," he confided one day, his voice trembling. "I am afraid the Lord will leave me and take everything away. If He took His power and His anointing from my life, would people still love me? No. If I were to become a Philip who speaks without the Lord's power and anointing, would people still listen to my voice? Of course not."

I was silent. I understood his fear. I had attended many of his revival services and seen the excessive response of the people.

The Public and Private Man

Comparing his demeanor in the pulpit with when he was in prayer before the Lord was like seeing two different Philip Mantofas. When he was ministering to a congregation of hundreds or thousands, he seemed so powerful. He boldly proclaimed the Word, and his faith was manifested to all who heard. When he exhorted people, his words were so saturated with faith that they brought many unbelievers to the altar for the Lord to touch, heal, and save them.

"Listen to me," he proclaimed boldly at one revival. "Whoever knows his brother is sinning before the Lord, but hinders him from coming to confess his sins, when you leave this room the blood of your brother will be on your head."

Many people knew that Philip Mantofa is the ambassador for Christ and the one bold enough to be the Lord's voice to the congregation. But when he was with the Lord, he was like the rest of us. He wept, pouring out his complaints and fears before Him.

Overcoming Fear

When Pastor Philip first decided to go to Bible school, he was afraid to tell his father because his father didn't know the Lord yet. He knew his calling, but he wasn't ready to face his father's reaction. For three days, he locked himself in his room and prayed. Knowing that his father was planning to visit him in Canada, he was tense and afraid. He consulted with his mother in Indonesia.

"Just be honest with him," she suggested.

His father's brief answer was beyond his expectations.

"OK, good, Philip. I will support you."

Philip was stunned by his father's answer. Maxi later described the expression on his brother's face like someone who had just been given ten Mercedes Benzes or Jaguars. Even Maxi agreed that it was a miracle, since at the time, his father didn't believe in the Lord or in any religion, for that matter. I wondered what power had softened his father's heart so that he so easily accepted his son's decision to become a pastor. But even more miraculous was the young man's own decision to go to Bible school and prepare for the ministry.

Maxi reflected on the transformation of his younger brother.

"I believe that my mother surrendering him to the Lord, made the difference in his life," Maxi said. "He had already taken too many risks. When he was small, he was sickly, and several times, he almost died. When he was still in junior high school, he was almost killed, and later, in Singapore, he had some close calls. Yet I believe that was all part of the Lord's plan to use him in amazing ways. I know Philip was not the only one in this world who had a life like that, but unfortunately, not everyone was brave enough to make a wise decision. Many people committed suicide, wasted their time at nightclubs, or became drug addicts. By God's grace, Philip surrendered to the Lord. Today the Lord has blessed our family because he was willing to surrender to Him and he prays for us every day."

My Life Principles

So then, King Agrippa, I was not disobedient to the vision from heaven (Acts 26:19).

Principle 1:
Obey Heaven

When I was small, I did not understand what a calling was. But I had a divine visitation when I was six years old, before I left for Taiwan. I had come down with a high fever. My mother was worried. She kept slapping my cheeks, asking, "Are you OK?"

Mama was always worried about my health because I was the weakest of her children. She also was afraid I would have another convulsion.

Although I was not yet born again, during my illness, I saw a vision. I knew about Jesus from Sunday school, but I didn't know Him personally in a real way. I had never seen anything like that vision. It was the beginning of God's call on my life.

I saw a huge, powerful stone rolling toward me, so close it was about to crush me. I didn't understand what this meant, but I was astonished. I stared at that huge stone rolling toward me without blinking, my eyes wide open. At that moment my mama slapped my cheeks and asked what was wrong. Suddenly, the vision vanished.

Although I was only a child, I knew it was a divine intervention. After a while, I forgot about the vision until the Lord Himself reminded me after I was saved. I asked a pastor about the meaning, and he said, "That was a solid, hard rock that would crush your life. But after the rock crushed your life, it would no longer be you who lived, but Christ who lived in you" (see Matt. 21:44; Gal. 2:20).

I understood from that vision and its meaning that God had deliberately chosen me, but not because I was worthy. He called me at such a young age that I did not yet know the difference between good and evil. Yet the Lord had already begun to speak to me about who He was. Perhaps because I was so young and didn't know Him yet, He revealed Himself to me in a veiled manner. Even so, the Lord spoke to me so that I would know it was He who called me.

Later, when I repented and was saved at age 18, the Holy Spirit said once again: "It is I who have called you." I know I am to follow Him, just like when He called His disciples and said, 'Follow Me'" (see Mark 1:17). Since that day, I abandoned all my hopes, desires, and aspirations, and I have followed Jesus.

At first, I quibbled a little with the Lord because I was not sure I was really hearing from Him. But then I discovered an unfathomable truth.

"You do not have the right to argue with Me. Your mother surrendered you to Me. She promised you to Me in a vow when you were sick."

I asked my mother if it was true. She had never told me or my father that she had dedicated me to the Lord. It was a secret promise between the Lord and my mother, spoken silently, in her heart. So she was surprised when I asked her about it.

"How did you know about that?" she asked.

"The Lord told me I could not run away from Him because I had been dedicated to Him by your vow."

Truly, the Lord chooses what is weak in human eyes to shame those who are wise (see 1 Cor. 1:27). Today, the sum of my life is nothing else but the fulfillment of His Word and His goodness. All I can do is to obey.

Principle 2: If Heaven Called Your Name, Your Heart Would Be Different

It is true that some preach Christ out of envy and rivalry, but others out of goodwill. The latter do so in love, knowing that I am put here for the defense of the gospel. The former preach Christ out of selfish ambition, not sincerely, supposing that they can stir up trouble for me while I am in chains. But what does it matter? The important thing is that in every way, whether from false motives or true, Christ is preached. And because of this I rejoice (Philippians 1:15-18a).

Because Heaven called my name, I have never, not for one second, doubted or wavered in my heart. So I cannot understand the thinking of people who take the call of the Lord lightly. I know He who called me, and He that called me is faithful (see 1 Thess. 5:24). Therefore I value His call. It is precious to me.

Some who are called to be pastors say, "I can't stand being a pastor anymore. I'm tired. I no longer have the strength."

Is there something I do not understand? How does such a thing happen? I have never had second thoughts about God's call. In my mind there has never been a plan B.

Some people say that every person called by God will pass through times of discouragement, pressure, or stress when they feel exhausted, weak, and want to quit. If he gives up, he forgets about God's call on his life. But if that person was really called by the Lord, he would not give up his calling, no matter how heavy the pressures or temptations (see John 10:11-14).

When I first began to minister in Ungaran, I was homesick. Sometimes I cried, turning my face to the wall and calling out for my mama and papa. My parents never knew I did that. The limitations of the facilities and other problems seemed to be hampering revival. But despite pressures and stress from every side, none of it could touch my certainty of Heaven's calling. I never forsook the path to becoming a pastor. It never crossed my mind to give up the goal of revival. The knowledge that Heaven called my name erased all doubt and indecision from my heart.

Even great temptations could not affect my calling. Because I knew I could not survive outside of the Lord's calling, I never even thought about it, even when I went through heavy trials. Difficult times make some people doubt their call. I too have experienced difficult times. But they are nothing in comparison to the reality of Heaven calling my name. His calling is forever in my heart.

> *What is more, I consider everything a loss compared to the surpassing greatness of knowing Christ Jesus my Lord, for whose sake I have lost all things. I consider them **rubbish**, that I may gain Christ* (Philippians 3:8).

Perhaps some will say, "Oh, Philip can say that because he has never experienced heavy trials." That is true in one sense. Compared to the Lord Jesus, my trials have been small. I have not yet shed my blood (see Heb. 12:3-4). But that doesn't mean I haven't been tested or endured my share of trials. It's as if the Lord placed a piece of Heaven in my heart and I cannot remove it. Heaven in my heart excludes doubt and indecision. They cannot remain.

Heaven called my name and that was crystal clear. Like the song, "As beautiful as a rainbow, as bright as the sun, Your promise is true and tested," God's call on my life is as sure as the sunrise and as plain as the clouds I see. Because of that, I cannot understand why many people deny, forsake, or doubt His call.

For people like that, my conclusion is that Heaven never called their names. They called their own names—because if Heaven had called their names, their hearts would be different.

Chapter 4

Forged in the Fire

PASTOR Hendra, Pastor Desi, and I picked up Pastor Johannes at the train station in Surabaya. Pastor Johannes was the pastor of Double R Church in the city of Semarang, on the north coast of Java. Over lunch, he told us a story about Pastor Philip's ministry in Ungaran.

Pastor Johannes' Testimony

"Pastor Philip, two friends, and I ministered in the village of Banyu Urip, near Semarang, in Central Java. The church did not own a car, so we rented one. From the moment we arrived, we were busy ministering from morning until night.

"Finally, the time came to sleep. We were surprised when we saw the place provided for us. There were neither soft mattresses nor mosquito nets. That night we slept on the floor on plaited mats. That was not our only challenge. The village had water problems, so we had to economize on our water use. We all decided not to bathe.

"When I saw the primitive conditions, I stole a glance at Pastor Philip, worried that he wouldn't be able to sleep that night. He was a ministry intern, fresh from seminary in Canada. I knew that his house in Canada was extravagant, with a Jacuzzi and a sauna. Even the long driveway had its own heater. The home he had left behind was a different world compared to the conditions in that little village.

"'Pastor Philip, are you able to sleep in a place like this?' I asked.

"'Jesus, the Son of God, the King of kings, was born in a humble manger,' he replied. 'If He could do it, why shouldn't I sleep in a place like this? If I can't sleep in a place like this, I am too arrogant.'

"Pastor Philip took his Bible and lay down on the mat. I watched as he tried to sleep without a single complaint. His humble heart touched me.

"When Philip, then 20, first came to Ungaran in 1994, he preferred to live in the dormitory rather than Pastor Samuel Handoko's home. The dormitory was in decrepit condition. His mattress was infested with lice, and he had to adjust to living in one room with 10 to 12 other people. The condition of the

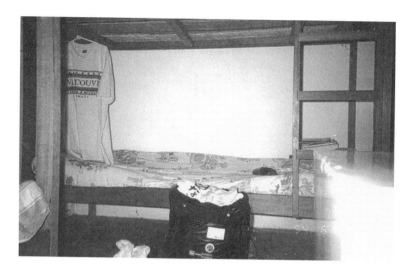

Pastor Philip's bed, Ungaran, 1994

bathroom and the toilet was awful. Despite the discomforts, I never heard him complain. The only reason he moved to Pastor Samuel's house was because his money kept disappearing, and Pastor Samuel pressured him to move."

The Miracle of Regeneration

Once Philip received Jesus, repented, and was delivered from the devil's shackles, he changed. As he sought the Lord, the fruit of patience became discernible.

> The fruit of the Spirit is love, joy, peace, patience, kindness, goodness, faithfulness, gentleness and self-control. Against such things there is no law. Those who

Graduation Day, Columbia Bible College, Canada

> *belong to Christ Jesus have crucified the sinful nature*
> *with its passions and desires. Since we live by the Spirit,*
> *let us keep in step with the Spirit* (Galatians 5:22-25).

His change began with little things, like the way he spoke and
handled his emotions. After a long process of testing and mold-
ing, he was no longer impatient and ungovernable. Philip had
been transformed.

> *Rid yourselves of all such things as these: anger, rage,*
> *malice, slander, and filthy language from your lips. ...*
> *since you have taken off your old self with its practices*
> *and have put on the new self, which is being renewed*
> *in knowledge in the image of its Creator* (Colossians
> 3:8-10).

The Family's Testimony

Philip's transformation touched his entire family, John said. "If our family is blessed by the Lord now, it is because of Philip's prayers."

John gave me an example.

"In 1999, I graduated from school in Canada and returned to Indonesia. That was a year of transition—a change from the world of school to the world of work. I went through a hard time. Philip said he would pray for me. I know I got through the transitions successfully because of his prayers. I believe he prayed not only for me, but also for our whole family."

He smiled as he observed, "If you're close to Philip for a while, your life will surely change. You'll wake up one day and realize that your attitudes and perspectives are different. That's what happened to me."

Maxi said he had seen firsthand how his brother used to erupt like a fire spattered with oil. It was almost impossible to extinguish his wrath. Now his family has learned patience because of his example. When he's faced with conflicts or opposition, instead of reacting to men, he brings his petitions to the Lord, picks up his guitar, and sings and worships Him.

"Now he's more patient than we are," said Hardi Mantofa, Pastor Philip's father. "In fact, what patience we have, we've learned from him. We used to get mad when others hurt us or criticized us. After Philip met the Lord, I saw him hurt by others several times, but he didn't get angry with the person who wounded him. The point is if we get angry, we remember Philip and immediately the anger dies," his father said.

A New Heart

Pastor Philip became patient because he was willing to be processed by the Lord. As he told the students at the church's Paul and Barnabas Mission School:

"My old heart has been destroyed in such a way by the Lord that it doesn't have the same shape anymore. But that new shape is not broken pieces patched back together. A damaged shard cannot be returned to its original shape. Once I submitted to the Lord's hand, the Lord who is the potter created in me a new heart" (see Ezek. 36:25-27; Luke 5:36-39).

Pastor Philip often spoke about how a servant did not have any personal rights. Once the Master purchased the servant, that servant lost all his rights, including his freedom. Because Pastor Philip understood that he did not have the right to demand anything or to protect himself, he developed patience, endurance, and long-suffering. The foundation for the fruit of the Spirit in his life was his surrender to the Lord.

My Life Principles

"Be perfect, therefore, as your heavenly Father is perfect" (Matt. 5:48). When I was baptized in Canada in 1992, the Lord spoke into my life, "I want you to become a man who pleases My heart."

Columbia Bible College

The story of David spoke so clearly to my heart that I made a commitment to become close to God. I want to be a man after God's own heart (see Acts 13:22). Since then, the Lord has been teaching me and He has given me a new heart—a heart for revival.

Principle 1: My Heart:
A Source of Perfect Peace for Others

> *And let the **peace of God** rule in your hearts, to which also you were called in one body...* (Colossians 3:15 NKJV).

One day, I attended a music team meeting at our church in Canada. Its purpose was to discuss a spiritual situation, but the environment quickly deteriorated and became extremely unspiritual. The atmosphere heated up as the team members confronted one another with their displeasure with their colleagues in the praise and worship ministry. My younger brother, John, who played guitar, also chimed in. I don't know what provoked our youth leader, who also led the praise and worship ministry, and was a song leader. Suddenly, he stood up in a challenging manner and ordered my brother to the front of the room.

The atmosphere got even hotter because they were both emotional. I really didn't expect what happened next because it happened so quickly. He suddenly threw a punch at my brother's face. John was only 14. This man was much older and far more spiritually mature than my younger brother. We were new at this church, but I was enthusiastic to serve from my heart. At the time, my only ministry responsibility was rolling up the microphone cables. I had just recently been saved, had repented, and had been filled with my first love, and I wanted to serve in any way I could without reward. But that day I felt disappointed and angry with this spiritually more mature brother. Right before my eyes he hit my younger brother, who was way too young to be a match for him.

John dodged his blow, but it landed on his neck. Startled and shocked, I also got emotional. Everyone stood up, trying to break up the fight. I leapt from my chair and grabbed the hands of the man who hit my brother. Unexpectedly, it crossed my mind to return his punch. It would have been very easy for me to hurt him. Those few seconds were the hardest temptation I ever passed through. I wanted desperately to please God's heart, but I also wanted to protect my younger brother.

In a flash my memory flew to Singapore, where not too long ago, a Taiwanese gang intentionally picked a fight with my younger brother. At the time, my brother used to return home at night alone. The gang lay in wait to chase him and beat him up. After discovering where they were, it didn't take long before I arrived at the place where nine of the Taiwanese gang members were gathered. They didn't expect me. I closed the door and locked it from the inside. Then I beat up those nine and, with the knife that I once carried everywhere, I almost killed the ring-leader. Afterward, I sought out their friends in the other apartments and beat them black and blue.

As the memory of that fight flooded my mind, I got ready to attack the man who had struck my little brother. Once again, I found myself in the middle of a conflict with my younger brother on one side and his aggressor on the other. I still remember the expression on John's face when he was asked to leave the room to speak to our pastor. He gave me a disappointed look, his stare seeming to accuse me of letting him down: "My older brother isn't the same. He doesn't protect me anymore."

My emotions exploded. In my heart, I plotted my revenge. *Everyone is busy breaking up the fight. This is my chance to attack him.*

But suddenly a voice spoke to my heart.

Ministry in Canada

"Do you want to bring revival? Do you want to be used by the Lord in mighty ways? Then you must have a heart that pleases God."

The Lord clearly spoke to my heart that a man whose heart pleases God is willing to pay the price, even in the face of injustice. I struggled for a long time before finally deciding to pay the price, no matter how great the cost, for the sake of maintaining a heart condition that pleased God. But my surrender was not yet complete. I tried to bargain with the Lord.

"OK, I'll forgive him. But after that I will go. I'll take my younger brother with me and we'll leave this church for good. There are lots of churches, not just this church. I'll just find another one."

At that moment the Lord severely reprimanded me.

"A person who gives up easily when faced with a challenge or who threatens to leave will never be used or blessed by Me. Someone who cannot finish what has been entrusted to him will not become great."

I was shocked. The Lord's words pierced my heart and echoed in its depths. I surrendered. "What do You want me to do, Lord?" (See Acts 9:1-6.)

There was no response. For a long time He allowed my question to stand without an answer. Worry began to attack me. I felt in danger of losing my intimacy with the Holy Spirit. So I rectified my previous words.

"OK, Lord. I will forgive him. I will not leave this church. But allow me to move to another department. I don't want to be in this department. And one more thing. Please don't force me to speak to him. I'll forgive him, but I never want to speak to him again."

This time the Lord really wanted to open my spiritual eyes.

"Philip, I am going to make you a worshiper of the Lord. So you may not move from this department."

I surrendered. I couldn't bargain anymore.

"OK. I will still serve in this department. I will not move to another church, and of course, I will forgive him. I will continue to submit to him in the praise and worship ministry."

It wasn't easy, but I wanted to learn to obey the commands of the Holy Spirit. Then, beyond all my expectations, the Holy

Spirit took my willing heart seriously and gave me an even more difficult command to follow.

"Philip, go find him. When you have found him, hug him and tell him you love him. Tell him you cannot hate him because he is your brother in Christ."

I threw myself down on the floor with a thud.

"What?! I love him? He is my brother in Christ? Did I hear You correctly? Lord, I think just forgiving him is good enough. Isn't Your request a bit excessive?"

Apparently the Lord demanded a high spiritual standard from me. At the time, I was not as spiritually mature or as respected as the man who hit my brother. Before that incident, I had admired him. He had been my mentor. It should have been he who came to me and threw his arms around me, saying, "It's over. Let's just forget about what happened. Please forgive me."

But I never heard those words from his mouth. The Lord kept urging me to embrace him, but I couldn't bring myself to do it right away. After a long time, I understood that the Lord knew what was in my heart, so He commanded me to humble myself and go to my brother first (see Matt. 18:21-22). He wanted me to have a radical heart for Him. He wanted to shape my character. That day I realized that the secret to being used by the Lord in an extraordinary way is found in a radical heart. Finally I found the man. He was in the church canteen with his fiancée. I knew it wouldn't be easy, but I embraced him because I did not want to lose my intimacy with the Holy Spirit. The risk of losing Him was more difficult to contemplate than the risk of being hurt by man.

"Lord, help me. Watch over my heart so I can be patient when I face this man," I prayed.

I approached him. When his fiancée saw me coming, she stood up and tried to protect him. She had the wrong idea. She thought I had come to retaliate. She was astonished when I pulled him to one side and embraced him, weeping.

"This is for You, Holy Spirit," I said in my heart. "You are the only reason I am doing this. I only want to please You. If You want me to do it again, I'll do it again. I am ready to pay the price for the sake of guarding my heart. What I am doing right now is not too costly compared to intimate fellowship with God," With tears, I said, "I cannot hate you because you are my brother in Christ."

A moment later we were both crying. I thought the problem was resolved. Apparently not. For then, the Lord began to use me in extraordinary ways. Following that reconciliation, my ministry was no longer rolling up cables or fetching the keyboard. My pastor entrusted me with the youth ministry, and the man who had hit my younger brother was asked to lead the ministry to college students and young professionals. We conducted our weekly meetings on the same day, but in different rooms.

One day, the Holy Spirit worked in an amazing way at a youth meeting I was leading. The meeting began with 10 people. As I began to preach, a visitation of God touched every person present. All ten of the young people fell headlong when they approached the front of the room. They were all weeping because of the Lord's touch. The next week the group increased to 20. Once again the Lord visited them. The following week, there were 40.

Seeing such rapid progress, this man filed a harsh protest. He accused me of being a "one-man show." He said I was monopolizing the ministry and did not give others opportunities to serve. His provocation succeeded and everyone rose up against me.

This continued until one day I faced a kangaroo court. I was forced to sit there without defending myself, surrounded by the people who had come to judge me. One by one, they made accusations against my ministry. Actually, these people did not intend to wound my heart. They were the ones whose lives had been restored by the Lord through me. The man who had struck my brother forced them to do it. Because they were afraid of him, everyone who had supported me turned around and opposed me that day while I was forbidden to speak even one word in my defense. This was very hurtful, and I was angry (see Ps. 35:11-12; 19-21). But the Lord had a different plan.

In 1997, I was visiting Indonesia when the Lord told me to return to Vancouver. I obeyed. Then He asked me to find that same brother again.

"Find him immediately. Apologize, because you grieved his heart."

I was incredulous. I didn't think I was wrong—he was. Why did I have to ask his forgiveness? At first, I rejected the request. But because it was the Lord who asked me to do it, I wanted to obey. I went to his fiancée's house. The fiancée opened the door, but he refused to meet with me. I did not lose hope. Around noon one day, I asked Irene to accompany me to his house. I entered the house while Irene waited in the car. He took a long time before he came downstairs. When he finally came down to see me, all I did was sit in the chair and cry.

"I am sorry," I told him. "I have grieved your heart many times."

He was surprised to hear what I had to say, but he answered coldly.

"Oh, yes. But perhaps I was wrong, too."

His reaction did not surprise me, but his next statement did. In the same tone of his voice, he complimented me.

"Philip, I must confess, in everything you are more spiritual than me."

I hugged him and said, "I love you."

I left the house, relieved that it was over. As I was leaving, the Holy Spirit clearly said to me, "As of today, you do not need to see him anymore. I know your heart. You are ready for revival."

When I returned to the car, I felt something heavy placed on my head—a crown. *"Blessed is the man who perseveres under trial, because when he has stood the test, he will receive the crown of life that God has promised to those who love Him"* (James 1:12).

I was about to start my car when the interior of the cabin filled with a light mist. Then I heard a voice say, "Return to Indonesia. You will see many young people repent. You will see your generation touched by God. I am willing to pass over a million people to anoint you because I know your heart. Because of your anointing, a generation of young people in Indonesia will experience revival."

The Lord would never again find me not reconciled with others, for He has called me to become Christ's peacemaker to others, even for those who have wounded my heart (see 2 Cor. 5:15-21).

In May 1998, riots in Indonesia traumatized sections of the country, resulting in unrest, violence, and the fall of President Suharto. Everyone discouraged me from going back. Yet I chose to believe the Lord, who promised to protect me, and I returned home to Indonesia. Although there was shaking and chaos in my country, that day I repeated over and over to myself that I was going home to a spiritual revival on a national scale. God's promise has proven true.

Principle 2: My Heart: A Source of Perfect Power for Others

> *It is God who arms me with strength, and makes my way perfect. He makes my feet like the feet of deer, and sets me on my high places* (Psalm 18:32-33 NKJV).

I want to climb His mountain and set my feet on the high spiritual peaks seldom reached by people. When I am on the heights, I will see things never seen by those who walk on ordinary paths. Those who choose to walk on ordinary paths see ordinary things. But those who walk on His heights will know God. The heights are a secret place between the Lord and me.

There, I walk with God as a friend. There, all criticism—and even human compliments—are but filthy rags (see Phil. 3:7-8).

Because my heart believes in my God, I can become a source of His power for others. He uses me to strengthen others' hearts by leading them to the One who is the source of all strength. Not for one second do I allow myself to feel my weaknesses. That doesn't mean that I have no weaknesses. In fact, it is because I am so weak in my flesh that I must become so strong in the power of the Lord. When I am weak, I go to the Lord, for my heart does not draw strength from others. I request power from the Lord, not from people.

God's Warrior

Eleazar was an ordinary man to whom God gave extraordinary power. Because of his boldness and strength, his works are mentioned in First Chronicles 11:12-14:

> Next to him was Eleazar son of Dodai the Ahohite, one of the three mighty men. He was with David at Pas Dammim when the Philistines gathered there for battle. At a place where there was a field full of barley, the troops fled from the Philistines. But they took their stand in the middle of the field. They defended it and struck the Philistines down, and the LORD brought about a great victory.

Why did Eleazar choose to stand with David when all of King David's soldiers ran away and left him? He alone believed when no one else did. Eleazar was the last man standing. He saw David standing alone in that barley field with an unsheathed sword. He easily could have fled with the other soldiers. But his love and respect for David filled his heart. He drew his sword and stood beside his king. And what happened? The two of them succeeded in defeating the Philistines and holding on to that field. Two men against an army? Yes! This is the principle I learned from the story of Eleazar: Just one person who walks with God can destroy and paralyze the enemy. I hold on to this principle even today. Let us have the mind of Eleazar. He was a source of perfect power for all of his friends and fellow soldiers because his eyes were focused on his king. Truly, one Eleazar was more terrifying to the foe than the entire army of Israel.

I desire to show the same allegiance to the Lord, my King. Even if I must stand alone, I choose to stand beside Him until all the harvest fields are seized from the devil's hands. I must be strong for the sake of those who are not. If just five minutes of my weakness means hell would have a chance to plunder God's people for five years, with His help, I will not allow it. Not in my lifetime.

Chapter 5

A Man of One Book

PASTOR Philip carried his Bible wherever he went. He studied it every morning before breakfast, reading each verse one by one, then contemplating in silence. After a few minutes, he repeated the same verses out loud.

Since I visited his office frequently while I was cowriting this book, I often saw and heard him reading his Bible. Sometimes, while walking up and down and around the office desk, he recited verses. I was curious.

"Pastor, why do you read the Bible so slowly? Just one chapter can take you more than an hour. I notice you pause often when reading. Must it be done that way?"

He smiled. "I try to picture what the Word says while I read it out loud," he said. "For me, Sianne, the Bible is God's love letter to me. I love reading it because its pages express God's passion. Now it's my turn to answer His letter. I want Him to know that I also love Him."

He handed me his Bible, its margins filled with handwritten notes. "It's like a diary," I thought, turning the pages. Pivotal life events, the Lord's promises to him, and the secrets of his anointing were written there.

With his permission, I brought home his Bible to help me write this book, and I showed it to my younger sister.

"Whose Bible is this filled with handwritten notes?" she exclaimed.

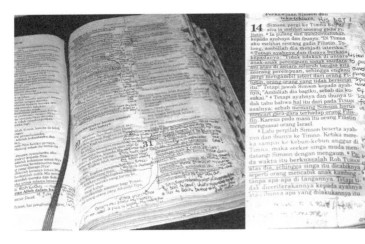

Philip's Bible

A few days later she began writing in her own Bible as well. Now all the margins of her Bible are filled with notes about the promises of God for her life.

"Imitating Pastor Philip, are you?" I teased. "You shouldn't. You should have your own walk and style."

She answered, "I believe if I imitate positive things, Pastor Philip will not object."

I had teased my younger sister—but then it was my turn to find my own walk with the Lord. As I watched the Lord working through Pastor Philip, I wanted to be like him. I tried to imitate him and the way he prayed and meditated on the Lord's Word. I thought if I couldn't imitate him, I'd never be used by the Lord like he was. I tried, but without success. I ended up getting frustrated with the Lord and with myself. I went to the church's prayer room and cried.

"Lord, I want to be like Pastor Philip. I've tried to pray and read the Word like him, but I can't. I've failed. I'm frustrated, Lord. I can't live like this. Does that mean I can't be used by You, Lord?"

The Lord answered me with a question. "Who told you to become like Philip?"

I was silent. The Lord had never told me to do that. I stopped crying and hung my head in shame.

"Philip is Philip," the Lord continued. "You are you. I will use you in the way I see fit, just as I will use Philip the way I see fit."

Although I no longer tried to imitate him, I have received many blessings from his life and example. For example, he asked me to read Psalm 119, the longest chapter in the Bible. That is how he passed along King David's passion for the Word of God to me.

Pastor Philip's life has influenced and inspired many people around him. Endang, an intercessor during his ministry internship at Maranatha Church in Ungaran, was also influenced by the way he reads his Bible. Endang eventually joined the senior pastoral staff in Ungaran.

Endang's Testimony

"One morning, I asked Philip, 'Why do I feel spiritually dry today?'

"'Did you read your Bible today?' he asked me.

"'Yes.'

"'How many chapters?'

"'Not too many, but I received a *rhema*.'

"'Suppose you eat a meal with your favorite food,' he said. 'It's delicious and nutritious, but, your portion is too small—just a little meat. Do you think that little bit of meat is enough to fill you up?'

"I saw his point immediately. 'I wouldn't be full, would I?' I answered softly.

"'Now, that is the answer,' he said. 'The fullness of your spirit depends on how much of the truth in God's Word you consumed today. Even though you got a *rhema*, since your daily portion of God's Word was too small, your spirit still feels hungry.'

"From then on," said Endang, "I disciplined myself to read God's Word daily."

I understood Endang. Sometimes it is challenging for believers to be consistent in the disciplines of reading the Word and prayer. While some may consider the Bible irrelevant, for those who love it, the Word represents the Lord Jesus Himself speaking to us.

Faith in the Living Word

When Pastor Philip let me take his Bible home for several days, I spent hours trying to understand his handwritten notes—some old, faded, and harder to read, others more recent entries. The faith, hopes, complaints, and even heartaches buried in those pages unlock the secret of his faith in the living Word. That was the key that opened my understanding of this man of God. Many of God's promises that are written in his Bible haven't happened yet. Others have been fulfilled. A sampling of his notes follows the Scripture portions below.

Samson's Bet, My Bet

> Samson went down to Timnah and saw there a young Philistine woman. When he returned, he said to his father

> and mother, "I have seen a Philistine woman in Timnah; now get her for me as my wife." His father and mother replied, "Isn't there an acceptable woman among your relatives or among all our people? Must you go to the uncircumcised Philistines to get a wife?" But Samson said to his father, "Get her for me. She's the right one for me" (Judges 14:1-3).

"Listen to your parents and find a spouse who has the same faith in Jesus."

> (His parents did not know that this was from the LORD, who was seeking an occasion to confront the Philistines; for at that time they were ruling over Israel.) Samson went down to Timnah together with his father and mother. As they approached the vineyards of Timnah, suddenly a young lion came roaring toward him. The Spirit of the LORD came upon him in power so that he tore the lion apart with his bare hands as he might have torn a young goat... (Judges 14:4-6).

"The Lord imparts the Holy Spirit, and gives supernatural abilities by His anointing."

> But he told neither his father nor his mother what he had done (Judges 14:6b).

"You don't have to tell everything to others."

> Some time later, when he went back to marry her, he turned aside to look at the lion's carcass. In it was a swarm of bees and some honey, which he scooped out with his hands and ate as he went along (Judges 14:8-9a).

"A characteristic of the anointing is that it remains. It can abide in the church, even in things that are dead."

When he rejoined his parents, he gave them some, and they too ate it. But he did not tell them that he had taken the honey from the lion's carcass. Now his father went down to see the woman. And Samson made a feast there, as was customary for bridegrooms. When he appeared, he was given thirty companions. "Let me tell you a riddle," Samson said to them. "If you can give me the answer within the seven days of the feast, I will give you thirty linen garments and thirty sets of clothes. If you can't tell me the answer, you must give me thirty linen garments and thirty sets of clothes." "Tell us your riddle," they said. "Let's hear it" (Judges 14:9b-13).

"Satan, I'll make a bet with you."

Then the Spirit of the LORD came upon him in power. He went down to Ashkelon, struck down thirty of their men, stripped them of their belongings and gave their clothes to those who had explained the riddle... (Judges 14:19).

"This is the *bet* (September 29, 1999)."

...Burning with anger, he went up to his father's house (Judges 14:19).

"Ablaze in holy zeal."

Sianne Speaks

Pastor Philip explained the bet to me.

"I wanted to do what Samson did," he said. "In the bet between Samson and the Philistines, Samson won. The bet between me and satan was exactly the same. The day I read that passage, I promised the Lord to bring 30 sinners to Him."

I thought he was living in a fantasy world, trying to twist the Lord's arm into making Samson's history his own. That's impossible, I thought. Philip Mantofa is not Samson! The story of Samson was past history. What did it have to do with this century?

But then he let me read his black daily organizer. In it he had recorded the outcome of his bet. What I read instantly destroyed my preexisting concepts. I realized he had the mustard seed kind of faith that could move mountains (see Matt. 17:20).

The notes in his organizer tallied the 30 souls he had won for the Lord in just one month and ten days, along with signs, wonders, deliverance, infillings of the Holy Spirit, and healings. Specific church meetings, dates, and the number of souls saved at each gathering were carefully notated. He had won the bet!

"The next target is 210 souls," he concluded in the organizer.

> Arise and thresh, O daughter of Zion; for I will make your horn iron, and I will make your hooves bronze; you shall beat in pieces many peoples; I will consecrate their gain to the LORD, and their substance to the Lord of the whole earth (Micah 4:13 NKJV).

As Pastor Philip applied the Bible with faith, the Word sprung to life and bore fruit. He walked with God believing that *"the Word of God is living and powerful..."* (Heb. 4:12 NKJV). He had been a warrior in the flesh. Now he was a warrior for the Lord. As Jesus said, *"From the days of John the Baptist until now the kingdom of heaven suffers violence, and the violent take it by force"* (Matt. 11:12 NKJV).

As I considered the year the bet took place, marked in his Bible as 1999, I marveled that he had won the bet so quickly. He was a newcomer at Mawar Sharon Church, known only as the son-in-law of Senior Pastor Jusuf Soetanto. He was new to the ministry, unrecognized, and still learning how to preach and serve. It seemed that God wasn't looking at resumes, but at hearts.

Faith Tested

As I pored over his Bible, I realized that his faith was a catalyst that sparked a spiritual awakening, raised up Mawar Sharon's youth and teen cell groups from their slump, and later, pioneered new churches in 2002 and 2003. His was a faith bathed with tears and intercessory groanings, a faith that energized him to boldly oppose the impossibility of everything happening around him.

In late June 2000, Mawar Sharon Church went through a devastating split. The worst damage was inflicted on the youth and teen cell groups. Most of the cell group leaders left, leaving behind about 200 wounded youth and teens. They lost their trust in their leaders. Cell groups were destroyed. But less than two months later, Philip wrote in his Bible that the Lord would shortly resurrect the youth and teens: Isaiah 27: Israel Saved, August 16, 2000.

Youth and Teen Revival

> *In that day, the LORD will punish with His sword, His fierce, great and powerful sword, Leviathan the gliding serpent, Leviathan the coiling serpent; He will slay the monster of the sea* (Isaiah 27:1).

"*His sword*—the Mighty Word of God. *He will slay the monster of the sea*—satan will be defeated by the revival to come. "

"*In that day*—'*Sing about a fruitful vineyard*'" (Isa. 27:2).

"The youth and teens of Mawar Sharon Church."

I, the Lord, watch over it; I water it continually... (Isa. 27:3).

"Holy Spirit outpouring."

> *I guard it day and night so that no one may harm it. I am not angry. If only there were briers and thorns confronting Me. I would march against them in battle; I would set them all on fire* (Isaiah 27:3-4).

"Circumstances and people who distress and destroy."

"*Or else let them come to Me for refuge; let them make peace with Me, yes, let them make peace with Me*" (Isa. 27:5).

"Pray. Pray."

> *In days to come Jacob will take root, Israel will bud and blossom and fill all the world with fruit* (Isaiah 27:6).

"*Take root*—Get serious with God. *Bud and blossom*—Expand the ministry and multiply the cell groups. *Fill all the world with fruit*—Fill the cell groups with souls through conversion of the multitudes."

By warfare and exile You contend with her—with His fierce blast He drives her out, as on a day the east wind blows (Isaiah 27:8).

"Wind of the Holy Ghost promised."

By this, then, will Jacob's guilt be atoned for, and this will be the full fruitage of the removal of his sin... (Isaiah 27:9).

"A great reward for holiness."

...When he makes all the altar stones to be like chalk stones crushed pieces, no Asherah poles or incense altars will be left standing....In that day the LORD will thresh from the flowing Euphrates to the Wadi of Egypt... (Isaiah 27:9,12).

"The Lord will visit His congregation."

...And you, O Israelites, will be gathered up one by one (Isaiah 27:12).

"Saving sinners one at a time."

And in that day a great trumpet will sound... (Isaiah 27:13).

"Revival will break out."

...Those who were perishing in Assyria and those who were exiled in Egypt... (Isaiah 27:13).

"The lost will come and be saved."

...will come and worship the LORD on the Holy mountain in Jerusalem (Isaiah 27:13).

"Many will worship the Lord in our youth and teen cell groups."

The Deaf Hear

Mark 7: Jesus heals a deaf man, August 19, 2000.

"Oh Jesus, allow Philip to do what You did and get the same result."

> Some people brought to Him a man who was deaf and could hardly talk, and they begged Him to place His hand on the man. After He took him aside, away from the crowd, Jesus put His fingers into the man's ears. Then He spit and touched the man's tongue. He looked up to heaven and with a deep sigh said to him," "Ephphatha!" (which means, "Be opened!"). At this, the man's ears were opened, his tongue was loosened and he began to speak plainly. Jesus commanded them not to tell anyone. But the more He did so, the more they kept talking about it. People were overwhelmed with amazement. "He has done everything well," they said. "He even makes the deaf hear and the mute speak" (Mark 7:32-37).

"*Deep sigh*—take a deep breath—gathering all the faith within Him and then releasing it in one word unto the sick parts of the body. *His tongue was loosened*—demon spirits. *He has done everything well. He even makes the deaf hear and the mute speak*— He makes all things well and perfect."

When Pastor Philip read this passage, he received faith to heal the deaf. The following day, Sunday, while he was preaching, a deaf man came to the front for the altar call. Pastor Philip placed two fingers in his ears and, while looking up, he took a deep breath, and said: "Ephphatha. Be open." Instantly the deaf person could hear.

In his organizer he wrote: "Deaf ears healed, healings plus deliverances."

Faith in Action

When I told Pastor Yosef Moro Wijaya about Pastor Philip's faith in the Bible, he told me about an outdoor revival service in Salatiga. People had already gathered on the outdoor field and the service was about to start when a hard rain interrupted the program. Everyone dispersed to seek shelter, including the praise and worship leader.

Pastor Philip came forward, took the microphone, and started singing a praise song repeatedly. People began to come forward toward the stage. Then what happened? The rain only lasted about 10 to 15 minutes. As soon as it stopped, Pastor Philip gave his microphone to the worship leader, and whispered in his ear, "Next time you're faced with a situation like this, use your faith" (see James 5:17). It didn't rain again and the program went on as scheduled.

My Life Principles

Oh, how I love Your law. I meditate on it all day long (Psalm 119:97).

Principle 1:
Let God's Word Be Your Daily Bread

My relationship with the Bible is so close that I believe the Lord sees it as a relationship with Him. Someone once asked me, "If you were stranded on an island alone and you could only choose one thing to bring, which would you take—one knapsack of food or your Bible? You must swim across with only one hand. So you can only take one of the two choices to sustain your life on that island."

I said to him: "You already know the answer, don't you? You know that I'll take my Bible, not the knapsack of food."

Why did I say that? Because if I take my Bible, I can read the Word. I know that even the ravens will bring me bread. But if I have a knapsack of food, but I do not have the Word from God's mouth, I am already cursed, a dead man.

Some people don't understand why I want to read the Bible over and over. When I was single and doing my ministry internship in Ungaran, I read at least ten chapters a day. Within a year, I had already read through the Bible several times."

Someone once asked me, "Don't you get bored reading the Bible over and over?"

Why would a Christian get bored reading his own holy book? Although the question surprised me, I answered, "This Bible is the evidence of my relationship with the Lord. So how is it possible I could be bored with Jesus, a Person who is so glorious? If I love Him, I also must love His Word because it is the voice of the Lord, the voice of a Person whom I love. Since I'm not bored with Jesus, I couldn't possibly be bored with His voice."

God's Love Letter

When I was dating Irene before we got married, I gathered several strands of her hair that had fallen out and put them in an album. I did that because I missed her so much. At the time, I was a student in Canada, and she was in Indonesia. Although the distance between us was great, I was close to her heart, and she was close to mine. So I kept every remembrance of her that I could, including her letters. And she kept mine.

If someone else read our letters, they wouldn't have understood them. They might even have asked, "What are these two talking about?"

That's what it's like when you don't have an intimate relationship with the Lord. If you don't love Him, when you read the Bible you'll say, "Gee, what is this Bible talking about?" And if you come across Scriptures about the building of the Holy Temple, which contain detailed building measurements, you'll probably wonder, "What is God talking about?"

But if you love the Lord, you'll love reading all His love letters. For me, the entire Bible is His love letter. Even when it comes to temple measurements, I read about them with love in my heart. If some who see my relationship with the Bible do not understand, it must be because they never really fell in love with the Lord. If they loved Him, they would read His love letter.

Some Christians believe they can't understand the Bible or grow to love and appreciate it unless they attend Bible school or seminary. But in reality, many theological students are not close to the Bible. They study *about* the Bible, not *the* Bible itself. Some people find my love for the Word a reproach. Others are inspired. Those who don't understand tend to criticize.

I used to have a multifunctional Bible cover where I also kept my toothbrush and toothpaste. When I traveled to villages to minister, my only supplies were the Bible, toothpaste, and a toothbrush. If the Lord wanted to send me anywhere, I was always ready. When I ministered in the villages, the Bible became my pillow. In the village of Krasak, my Bible was the pillow for my head. I slept on a cold cement floor on an old rice sack. The next day, when I woke up, the first thing I did was brush my teeth and read my Bible. Then I went to work for the Lord. I preached, prayed for people, and went out to evangelize in the surrounding villages.

I do not idolize my Bible. I realize that it's just a book. What I love is not the book, but the words of God, His commands inside its covers. When the Lord Jesus rebuked the devil, who tempted Him in the desert, He said, "*It is written...*" (see Matt 4:1-11). The Bible contains the written eternal truths of God. But we cannot love His Word if we do not love our Bible. However, we should be careful not to worship the Bible. It's not a charm. We are to just live out God's written truths in it. That is my principle.

Principle 2:
Make the Bible Your Most Important Book

After my return to Indonesia from Canada, I had occasion to observe the world of Christianity in Indonesia. I had studied theology at Columbia Bible College in Vancouver, but was thirsty for more knowledge about the things of the Lord. I was young, naïve, and gullible, and the believers around me seemed very knowledgeable.

At that time, reading spiritual books was the latest trend among the Indonesian churches, and many deemed them helpful to their spiritual growth. I felt out of step with my peers. The Lord's servants, especially the youth my age, were satisfying their thirst for knowledge by diligently reading spiritual books.

There was only one book in my life. At that time, aside from required reading for school, I really only wanted to read the Bible. But when I noticed other people's infatuation for spiritual books, it piqued my desire to read them like everyone else.

In Surabaya, it seemed that Christians there revered spiritual books more than their Bibles. The Bible wasn't real for them. They saw it as an outdated textbook. When I talked to them about the Scriptures, they seemed uninterested.

One day I prayed, "Lord, You know I love You and I love Your Word. You know that right now this Bible is the one and only book in my life. But Lord, allow me for the next year to draw knowledge from spiritual books. I feel out of place with my peers, especially other young servants of the Lord. They seem to be getting spiritual knowledge from these books. I don't own even one, but my friends have so many. I won't get anywhere if I just keep reading Genesis to Revelation all the time. Haven't I already read this Bible from cover to cover? So allow me to not read the Bible for one year. During that year I'll study all the good spiritual books that people say can bring us closer to You and help us be used by You in extraordinary ways."

The Lord didn't answer me. But I badgered him with that prayer.

"Just one year. After that I'll return to my former relationship with the Bible. I'll use that year as a break from the Bible. I don't want the others to leave me behind."

After I said, "Amen," I forsook my Bible and locked it in my desk drawer. But the next day a miracle happened.

The Bible that Seeped Oil

Fortunately, the following day, I wanted to get something I had left in my Bible. I don't remember if it was a letter or a note. When I opened the cover, I was amazed. My Bible was wet, soaked with oil. The oil saturated my Bible, filling the air with fragrance.

"Who spilled oil on my Bible?" I wondered.

I thought someone had spilled oil because I used to carry anointing oil everywhere. But it had been a long time since I carried anointing oil. Then where did this oil come from?

I was perplexed because I had locked the drawer. I tried wiping the oil off my pants, but my tan pants were ruined because the oil stain wouldn't come out. Finally, with a little hard work, I succeeded in wiping up the oil until the Bible was dry. It was a little wet, but not as much as when I first found it. Then I returned my Bible to the drawer and locked it.

The next day, curiosity compelled me to check again. I really wanted to know who had spilled oil on the Bible. I unlocked the drawer, and opened the Bible. It was saturated with oil, just like the day before, soaking wet and sticky. I was not brave enough to open it again.

Suddenly I felt the Lord's anointing and presence in my room. Trembling, I asked Him, "Why did that happen, Lord? What do You want to tell me?"

I wiped the oil from my Bible and put it on the table. Its fragrance pervaded my room. Trembling, I knelt at the Lord's feet.

"What is Your message behind this?"

I knew the Lord never did anything without a purpose. It was vital that I learn what it was. That day the Holy Spirit clearly spoke to my heart.

"Philip, do you want to be close to God?" He asked. "Do you want Me to use you? Do you want to become an anointed man of God? That will not happen through other spiritual books, but through My Word."

The Lord opened my eyes. I realized my prayer and decision to leave the Bible for one year for the sake of reading other spiritual books was wrong. My thinking that those books would make me more anointed and in step with others was erroneous.

The Lord showed me that if I wanted to be anointed by God, stay close to Him, and be used by Him, I must meditate on His Word day and night and do whatever is written in it (see Josh. 1:8).

After the Lord opened my eyes, I realized that the others were the ones who were out of step with God, not me.

Reading and putting into practice God's written Word is the way we develop a relationship with Christ. The highest authority is God's Word, not our experience, no matter how spectacular, and not other spiritual books.

Because the Lord loves me, He reprimanded me. He became jealous because my intimacy with the Bible was threatened when I began to care about people's opinions. Apparently, the Lord is so happy to see me close to Him through His Word that He prepared a miracle that prevented me from taking the wrong path and brought me back to the truth. He sent that miracle so that I would never be far from the Bible. When the Holy Spirit revealed this to me, I wept and firmly took hold of my Bible.

"For the sake of making Myself known to the Israelites, I poured water from a stone. Today, to make you understand, I poured oil from your Bible, so you will know that there is no other book that is anointed like the Bible, which contains My written words. This book is truth for those who believe and lay hold of it."

After the Lord revealed this truth to me, the oil stopped flowing. A month after the oil ceased, my Bible peeled apart from the front to the back cover, so I exchanged it for the Bible I use now.

I hid that Bible and let people think it was lost because I didn't want it to become a fetish idolized by others. I understand now that the Bible is the anointed book because the written words of the Lord are within it.

Today, when I have time, I read spiritual books as supplemental reading. For others, spiritual books are their primary reading material, and the Bible is a supplement. Some people interpret the Bible through the other books they read. But for me, the Bible is the lens through which I read other books.

The Lord built my ministry on the foundation of the truth of God's Word. The foundation of my life is His written Word, and the revelations I receive come purely from God's Word. My foundation is firm.

Chapter 6

Irene Forever Will Be

"I fell in love at first sight with Irene, Sianne," Pastor Philip told me. "And after we dated for a while, she said the same thing. The first time she saw me, she knew I was the one."

When he described how he waited for the woman he loved to love him in return and his longing when they were separated by a long distance, I knew this young pastor adored his wife, Irene Saphira, the daughter of Jusuf Soetanto, senior pastor of Mawar Sharon Church.

"I wrote this song for Irene when I was in Canada and she was in Indonesia. I actually sang it on our wedding day, but I didn't get to finish due to time constraints. So today, five years later, I want to finish singing the song to her."

He prepared his surprise well. He chose a keyboard accompanist and ordered a bouquet of flowers. Then he picked up his guitar and started singing, "Irene, Forever Will Be" from the heart, practicing without embarrassment. This was a side of him seldom seen in public.

How can I tell you
How much I want to be your best friend forever
How can I show you how precious you are to me
So precious forever you will be
Will you give your love to me?
Will you give your heart to me?
Irene forever will be

Just Married

Just married, 1999

Maintaining a marriage in the whirl of a busy schedule is not easy. One week Pastor Philip could preach at revival services for three days on Sulawesi Island, and five days later, minister in Sumatra Island, 1800 miles away. More satellite churches are being founded, which means more work to do. The move of God is spreading rapidly, so he meets with pastors two to three times a day.

In any given month, the days he's home in Surabaya can be counted on one hand. Likewise, Irene is not a traditional pastor's wife with responsibilities only on Sunday. She is a business-woman with responsibilities in the marketplace. With schedules like these, how do they maintain their relationship? I didn't know until I heard Irene Saphira's story over a vanilla latte at Starbucks.

Irene's Story

"The first time I saw my husband was at church sitting beneath the balcony. He was sitting on the corner. A voice in my heart said, 'He is the one for you.'

"I was only 14. We didn't meet that day, but a few weeks later, someone introduced us at a prayer meeting. In the following days, he often telephoned. Our conversation was casual. After several months, his conversations began to get more personal. At one point, I drew back, but he did not retreat. I noticed how bold he was when he was sure he was on the right track. But I was grateful that he never said, 'Thus says the Lord,' as Christian youth in love are apt to do.

"Whenever I had a problem, he was a faithful friend who listened to my complaints and was always there when I needed him.

His patience impressed me. After a long time, affection for him grew in my heart. Years later, in 1995, we started dating officially.

Long-Distance Courtship

"We dated for four years. We seldom met except when he returned to Indonesia from Canada two to three times a year. Most of our courtship was by long-distance telephone three to four times a week. We both understood the risks of a long-distance romance—they are seldom successful.

"Philip had many female friends in Canada who were interested in him, and in Indonesia, many male friends were chasing me. Our greatest challenge was to maintain our commitment, which we guarded in a unique way—with special diaries. We exchanged our diaries by mail once a month. That way, we kept in touch with each other's ups and downs. So when we met, we felt close to each other and our conversation easily picked up where our diaries had left off.

"When we got married, we didn't experience many difficulties because we already knew each other's personalities well. Our dating was not very physical in nature because our goal was to know each other's inner person first. So we minimized physical touching as much as possible. We both knew that purity is the way to a godly marriage.

"After being married for many years, we are happier now than when we were dating. We believe the main reason is because we made an investment in our marriage through holy dating. As a result, we reaped a great reward. I believe this blessing will also be passed down to our children and grandchildren.

"God has given me the best parents-in-law in the world. My in-laws love me, accept me no matter what, and understand our relationship. I love and regard them as my own mama and papa. We never use the words 'your mama and papa.' We only say 'mama and papa.' Likewise, my parents are quite fond of him."

A Foundation of Trust

"Although my husband fell in love with me at first sight, initially, I was cautious and a little afraid of his persistent advances. Despite my reserve, in the four years that he pursued me, I never saw him give up hope or shift his focus to pursue another woman. I also noticed that this man was very strict about holiness. Even now, when we visit Hong Kong, for example, there are sexually provocative images everywhere. He strictly guards his commitment to purity, walking with his head bowed and eyes averted. If such images appear on TV, he immediately changes the channel without glancing at the screen. It was because of his steadfast commitment to holiness that I finally gained the confidence to decide: 'I will entrust my life to this man.'

"While we were dating, he admitted, 'I actually never wanted to get married. It was only since I met you that I changed my mind. Even if you say no, I will wait for you. But if in the end, you don't want to marry me, I will return to my former position and concentrate on my ministry.'

"'OK, prove it,' I answered.

"And he did. Once he began to say he loved me, I asked him the same question I'd asked other men who pursued me. 'Why do you love me? What is your reason?'

"'I love you because you love the Lord and your family. When I'm close to you, I want to be close to the Lord.' His answer touched my heart."

Handling Conflicts

"While conflicts seldom occur in our married life, they happen from time to time because we are both very strong-willed.

Philip, Vanessa, and Irene

We are both leaders and busy in our own fields. We normally spend time together in the evenings. In the morning our time together is brief because we have to go to work. So we must respect each other's time constraints.

"There are times when our character differences come to the forefront. We have different styles of resolving problems. I prefer to calm down first so I can choose my words carefully. Then I return to the conversation to speak my mind. My husband, on

Pastor Philip and Vanessa, Canada

the contrary, feels he must sit down and immediately resolve the problem. Because of these two different approaches, many conflicts arose, especially at the beginning of our marriage. Then we thought of a way to resolve conflicts without hurting each other's feelings.

"We agreed that if one gets upset first, the other must give in. That means if my husband is angry, I must give in and let him make the decision. I have to keep quiet while calming my thoughts and emotions and speak with self-control. But if I'm the one who is angry, then my husband must give in and allow me to make the decision. Ever since we agreed to handle conflicts this way, we have not had any significant problems in our marriage.

Share Your Husband With the Lord

"I am aware of the difference between a pastor's wife and one whose husband is not called to the ministry. I always tell the ladies whose husbands are full-time or part-time at church, 'Whether we like it or not, we share our husbands with the Lord. There are times when we have to release our husbands to serve the Lord. Do not hamper that. Don't come between your husband and the Lord.' When my husband ministers, I say, 'Go ahead. I'll handle things here at home.' I feel better if I support rather than dominate him, and he appreciates it too."

Our Children

"After we had been married for six months, I wanted to have a baby. We took our desire to God in prayer for six more months. The fruit of our faith was Vanessa's birth. Everyone says she looks exactly like her daddy. After that God blessed us with two boys: Jeremy and Warren.

"Although their father is a pastor, we encourage our children to just be themselves. My experience as a pastor's child convinced me that this was the best approach. I used to be naughty at school, and the principal often rebuked me harshly.

"'You are a pastor's child and yet you act like this.'

"That made me question, 'Who wants to be a pastor's child, anyway?' I knew about Papa's ministry, but the real meaning of serving the Lord was not yet alive in my heart.

"I admired Mama, who visited the school one day and said cooly to the principal, 'Let my child be herself. My husband was the one who received a calling to become a pastor, not my child. Let her grow up normally, like her peers. Let her learn from experience like other teens her age. Please accept her for who she is.'

"Because of what I went through, I want my children to grow like other children. Until they understand the meaning of their own calling, and experience it for themselves, we will simply teach them to walk in the ways of the Lord."

Define Priorities

"We are both busy, but that's no excuse not to set time aside for all of us. We have made family a priority. Twice a year we go on family vacations overseas. During normal weeks, we set aside a family day. We don't ever want our children to feel that their daddy is close to the Lord and the church, but not to them. I don't want my husband to become like many pastors who feel guilty when they spend time with their families.

Philip, Vanessa, and Irene

"Our sanctified 'work hard, play hard' principle is: When

we're at work, we work as unto the Lord (see Col. 3:23). But on family vacations or days off, we spend quality time with no work, business, or ministry whatsoever. On those days, we give our best time to our children and to one another.

"My husband and I also enjoy time together during business trips overseas. Then the two of us can discuss deep personal things and learn in detail how the other is doing. Those are times of refreshing and restoration in our relationship.

"Although our family vision is to serve the Lord, we don't want our ministry to succeed, but our family to end up in disarray. We don't want our children to feel like orphans. We want to live what we preach from the pulpit."

Let's Pray for Daddy

"I have often observed that when my husband is about to engage in major ministry with a significant impact, the devil opposes him. At such times, our family becomes the devil's target. We used to take these things lightly. But Vanessa, who is very spiritually sensitive, was often attacked.

"On several occasions before a revival service, I felt like the devil was choking me so hard that it was difficult to breathe. Simultaneously, Vanessa began to cry hard. Now, before a ministry event, we always ask the prayer team to support and cover us in prayer.

"As soon as Vanessa could talk, I taught her to pray for her daddy. 'Vanessa, let's pray for Daddy. Come on, close your eyes.'

"Vanessa closes her eyes and follows my promptings. 'Lord Jesus, we want to pray for Daddy....'"

My Life Principles

The Foundational Principle:
Holiness Is Beautiful

> *Worship the LORD in the beauty of holiness* (Psalm 29:2b NKJV).

How do we maintain purity during courtship? Nowadays, the devil has successfully deceived many to believe that holiness is a synonym for unhappiness. For years, the devil has used the media to disseminate values that contradict the Word of God. Almost every medium—television, movies, and print—suggests that being pure is a drag. This mindset encourages young people to express their love without boundaries. Young people seek freedom, not rules, in their relationships, and the media knows just the right way to package messages that provoke that desire by promoting sex outside of marriage. It's surprising how easily people believe this lie. Don't they know that holiness is beautiful?

What the world calls "freedom" is actually bondage to sin (see Rom. 6:16-21). The truth is, guarding your holiness will never rob you of your happiness. On the contrary, it will be value added to your relationship. The Lord's truth does not destroy enjoyment—it gives you real freedom, not the false freedom that the world teaches, which only leads you deeper into bondage. Holiness is not the same as legalism.

If you are a Christian who is violating or struggling against God's commandment to be pure, you are being tested. If all you can think about is dating spiced by sex, the awesome call on your life that God has prepared for you will slip away and be lost without your knowing it. Why? Because you have forgotten the true purpose of your life. This happened because you have not heeded God's road marks (see Ps. 25:4; Prov. 4:26; 14:12). Then your life becomes empty, and the emptiness in your soul deepens because you are following the wrong road signs and the wrong voice. If you want to find true happiness, learn to trust in God's voice, like sheep who hear the voice of the shepherd.

Five Principles for Holy Dating

Principle 1:
Date Only the One You Will Marry

The Bible does not address dating, perhaps because in those days, parents arranged their children's marriages. However, the Bible does make it clear that purity and holiness are foundational to Christian living. Paul said that if we have the Holy Spirit and the mind of Christ, we do not live according to the flesh (see Rom. 8:5-16). The apostle further explained that one who begins his walk by the Spirit must not finish by the flesh (see Gal. 3:3). If you are born again and the Holy Spirit dwells in you, you are accountable for your choices.

If you love someone, you should also respect him or her. Love is more than feelings—it also means responsibility. What kind of love gives us enduring satisfaction? Responsible love. Love between a man and a woman is holy, so it should be valued. If you appreciate your partner while dating, you will appreciate him or her even more when you're married. When you date with this attitude, the person becomes valuable in your eyes. So when you think about dating, make sure that mutual respect is part of the relationship, since he or she will become your life partner. Look at that person not only as someone you fell in love with, but also as the partner who will accompany you to the end of your life.

The Right Start

When I fell in love with Irene and began to build a serious relationship with her, I made a choice: "This is the woman I love and will marry. I will live with her my entire life." If you cannot make that kind of commitment, it is better not to date.

The Right Timing

> *Daughters of Jerusalem, I charge you: Do not arouse or waken love until it so desires* (Song of Sol. 8:4).

This Scripture can be applied to the right time to begin dating. Before making that decision, ask yourself when you will marry. Once you know the answer, you can start to think about the right time to develop a closer relationship.

After I graduated from high school, but before I entered Bible school, Pastor Sonny, my pastor in Canada, asked me if I had thought about when I would get married. I was only 18. Though his question surprised me, I felt it needed to be answered, as the Bible teaches us to involve the Lord in our life plans.

"Pastor, I want to get married when I'm 25."

"What is your reason? Why 25?" he asked.

My answer was practical. From age 18 to the next four years, I'd be in Bible school. At 22, I would graduate. The following year I wanted to serve Jesus on the mission field. That meant that from 22 to 23, I wanted to give everything—my time, energy, life, and tears to Jesus. I wanted to be all out for Him and Him alone. From 23 to 25, together with my prospective wife, I could begin preparing for marriage. But before marriage, I would start a business so I could be self-supporting in the ministry without having to rely on the church.

It turned out exactly as I'd planned. I got married when I was 25.

While some people date for a long time before they get married, those cases are the exception. Why build your future on an exception? If you're not ready for a serious commitment, consider not dating yet. Falling in love is beautiful. But do not set that love in motion or develop it before its time.

Principle 2:
Cultivate the Fruit of the Spirit

By their fruit you will recognize them. Do people pick grapes from thornbushes, or figs from thistles? Likewise every good tree bears good fruit, but a bad tree bears bad fruit. A good tree cannot bear bad fruit, and a bad tree cannot bear good fruit. Every tree that does not bear

> *good fruit is cut down and thrown into the fire. Thus, by their fruit you will recognize them* (Matthew 7:16-20).

I have observed that many churches don't counsel their young people about clear standards for dating. Yet in every church where prophetic revival is breaking out, young people are falling in love. When they are in love, they often claim they've heard the voice of the Lord confirming their relationship. Some even say that they received a vision or heard His voice audibly. The name of the Lord is often misused this way, even though the Bible clearly warns us not to use His name in vain.

The principle that protects us from deception is actually quite simple. Do not boast about the tree, "This tree is from the Lord," but show us the fruit and we will immediately recognize what kind of tree it comes from (see Luke 6:43-44). What matters is that we glorify the Lord in our love relationships. So during dating, it's important to pay attention to character-building and the readiness to build a lasting relationship before marriage. Holy dating should produce godly progress in our walk, not backsliding.

Acknowledge the Laws of Your Body

From the time I was six years old in Taipei, Taiwan, I trained in martial arts. There I learned one of the principles of karate: "You cannot subdue your opponent if you do not learn to respect his strength."

In one karate competition, I fought someone nicknamed the "master" by his friends. My karate was already pretty good, and

I was fast. As I faced him, I felt arrogant and overconfident. I did not consider my opponent's strength, but I trusted in my own. That was the cause of my loss. He easily incapacitated me in five seconds. That day I learned the need to appreciate the strength of my opponent. If you want to defeat your enemy, the first thing you need to do is to respect his strength. I never lost again.

The same principle applies to dating. If you want to successfully control your flesh while you're dating, you must first respect the laws of your flesh. If you succeed, you will be able to guard your purity until marriage.

Some people ask if Christians who are dating can kiss on the lips. If you're dating in the right way and both sets of parents know about your relationship, it's my opinion that kissing on the lips is permissible. But it's advisable to limit the kiss to about two seconds, because lingering kisses can easily develop into foreplay. This can set a couple on the dangerous course of intercourse before marriage.

When I was dating Irene, I discovered a safe way to express love without being trapped in the snare of sin—a two-second kiss, and only when we said goodbye.

Also respect the sanctity of the bedroom. Before marriage, never enter the bedroom of someone you are dating, not for any reason.

How about embracing? Some churches do not allow Christians to kiss or embrace when they are dating. Others offer no advice on this topic to couples. Our solution was a special embrace in which only our heads touched, but from the shoulders down there was plenty of distance to separate us.

Shun Idolatry

While I was dating Irene, the Holy Spirit spoke to me about idolatry: "Whatever you idolize during dating, you will not enjoy in marriage." If you idolize sex while you're dating, you won't enjoy it as much when you're married. You may end up being more attracted to others rather than to your spouse. What you sanctify during dating, you will enjoy when you marry.

Your Reward:
The Wedding Day Blessing

The goal of cultivating the fruit of the Spirit during dating is so that we are worthy for His blessing to descend from Heaven on our wedding day.

> See that no one is sexually immoral, or is godless like Esau, who for a single meal sold his inheritance rights as the oldest son. Afterward, as you know, when he wanted to inherit this blessing, he was rejected. He could bring about no change of mind, though he sought the blessing with tears (Hebrews 12:16-17).

The prayer to bless the marriage is not just a religious ritual—it symbolizes the blessing of the Lord Himself and His Church over a man and a woman who bind themselves to each other at the altar. When a pastor extends his hands over the bride and groom, a supernatural blessing descends on their home and family for the rest of their lives.

But many people do not see it as a blessing from the Lord. The consequence is often years of marriage spent in tears, as if the very earth opposes them. The Bible says, "*Do not be deceived: God cannot be mocked. A man reaps what he sows*" (Gal. 6:7). You may be able to manipulate believers or churches, but you cannot manipulate God into blessing you. You can lie to the pastor, but you can't lie to God. So don't despise the holy marriage blessing. Without it, God's blessings will not rest on your home.

The marriage blessing is also a financial blessing. It means the Lord will protect your life and "ground," i.e., the fruit of your labor. God will not oppose you as He did Adam when he sinned (see Gen. 3:17). My wife and I are happy and fulfilled in our marriage because the ground we walk on is not iron and the heavens are not brass.

Finally, the wedding blessing is also for your children and grandchildren. When Vanessa was one year old, I saw her holding up one of her toys, a teething chain. She raised the chain over her head with both hands. Suddenly I remembered the chain I always carried to revival services to illustrate breaking bondages. I raise the chain high above my head with both hands when giving an altar call, proclaiming freedom from bondage. That chain has been the mute witness of the repentance of 35,000 souls in three years, with 9,000 of them added to our church.

When I saw Vanessa holding up the toy chain, I laughed. She looked so funny. But the Holy Spirit spoke to me.

"Don't laugh. This is not a coincidence. The best I put into your life will be passed on to your children and to their children through the holy blessing you received on your wedding day. Years from now you will see that your children have inherited the best from their mother and father. If you and your wife had sown evil, you would have reaped death, and that would also be passed to your children. What you sow is not for yourself alone. Your children will be a reflection of you."

Principle 3:
Honor Your Parents

> *Honor your father and your mother, so that you may live long in the land the LORD your God is giving you* (Exodus 20:12).

Affirmation of a marital relationship should not come only from a spiritual leader. Your parents and your spouse's parents should also approve. Their blessing will greatly influence the happiness of your home.

Why is there disharmony in a home? Why do husband and wife live together but quarrel continuously? It may surprise you, but if you and your spouse don't show respect to your parents, it will ultimately affect how you respect each other. You may not be aware that dishonoring your parents sows a seed of rebellion in your own household.

However, if your parents do not respond wisely to your relationship or judge it fairly according to God's Word, pray and try to win their approval in positive ways. God is on the side of those who do right, and He will give them the victory in the end.

Principle 4:
Honor Your Pastor and Spiritual Leaders

If your parents have blessed your relationship, but you don't respect your pastor and elders, you may face trials and loss as a result. Hebrews 13:17 states, *"Obey your leaders and submit to their authority. They keep watch over you as men who must give an account."*

If you have hidden your romantic relationship from your pastor, the spiritual covering over your most intimate human relationship has been removed. After you're married, all the members of your family will be in danger of a compromised spiritual walk. You may have a harmonious home, but without the blessing and covering of your pastor and spiritual leaders, your household is at risk for coming under attack. Those who violate the authority of their spiritual leaders risk compromising their family's love for and walk before the Lord, the presence of the Holy Spirit, the spirit of submission, and the biblical values that strengthen the foundation of their homes. Therefore, seek the guidance and approval of your pastor in your dating and marriage decisions, for his blessing will greatly influence the spiritual growth and well-being of your family.

A pastor should be neither prophet nor policeman, but a father and best friend. Though he should guide like a father, he does not have the right to determine whom you should fall in love with and marry. That decision is between you and the Lord, not you and your pastor. Your life is ultimately your responsibility before God.

But pastors, do guide your spiritual children. When the time is right, the parents on both sides agree, and the couple has proven to be responsible, and their spirituality has been tested, affirm them. Become best friends with your spiritual children.

As a pastor, if I affirm a couple's relationship, I will watch over them as best I can so they do not fall into sin, so they stay pure and attain a holy marriage. But if they fail to guard their purity and come to me, I will not judge them, but guide and restore them. That does not mean that I have an easygoing attitude toward sin. If necessary, I would not hesitate to suggest a break-up. I believe a father has the authority to discipline his children.

Principle 5:
Love Unconditionally

Unconditional love is the foundation for every godly relationship. Whether you are single or married, put God's love in first place. Find your soul mate in God's family. These are my suggestions:

For those who don't have a boyfriend or girlfriend, don't be anxious. The Lord prepares the best in His time. Enjoy your singleness in the Lord—there's no need to rush. Pray and socialize in a wholesome way so in the end you'll marry your best friend. Guard your attitude, speech, and appearance. *"Do not allow what you consider good to be spoken of as evil"* (Rom. 14:16).

For those who have a boyfriend or girlfriend, remember that unconditional love, like the *agape* love of God, is the source of happiness, not passion or infatuation. Many couples who begin their relationship with excessive passion end up with unfaithfulness and bitterness. Their love fails in the middle of the road. The core of a committed relationship is not so much the love we receive, but our understanding of the strengths and weaknesses of our partner. Understanding and supporting each other is the road toward true happiness. So let attraction develop into unconditional love and the grace to accept your partner as he or she is.

For those already married, keep loving each other unconditionally until Jesus Christ comes back. Then your love will be eternal in Heaven.

Balancing Family and Ministry

When I am in the presence of God and His glory, I belong to Christ alone. I am a son to no one, a husband to no one, a daddy to no one, a brother to no one.

When I give an altar call, my grandmother and aunts could be the first to come to the front. Then I am the Lord's servant and they are God's field, His congregation, His people. So there is a difference spiritually when I wear the robes of Christ's anointing, even when my family is in the congregation. But when I'm alone with my family, I'm just the Philip they've always known. I don't change the way I talk or joke with my brothers. The only difference is the change in my character and maturity in Christ.

These two realities are like two different poles. One pole is the anointing and the other is family. The Lord created both, just as

Philip, Vanessa, and Irene

he made the North and South Poles. In both of these poles, we must become a blessing.

When I'm with my family, do not call me an apostle or any other title. That makes me uncomfortable. When I go home, I am the husband of Irene Saphira and the father of my children. When I get together with my extended family, I don't wear the robes of anointing or of my pastorate. I act and speak as a child and a brother.

Why do I make a point of this difference? Because I have seen many of the Lord's servants lose their good relationships and communication with their families. This problem begins when they forget to take off their anointed robes at home. As a result, many pastors' children do not follow in their fathers' ministries because they have lost the father figure in their lives.

I do not want my children to lose their father figure. When I play with them, I don't need to remind them that I am the Lord's servant. They can hear from others that their father is a pastor. I only want them to know me as their father, who plays with them whenever they want, who is beside them when they need him, a papa who loves the Lord.

But when I am under the anointing of the Lord, I cannot do that. Suppose my children are among others at a children's revival service. I can't pay special attention to them because they're my children. All the children at that revival service are my priority. That way, they will all be served well. I do not want my ministry to succeed while my family is destroyed. When I am at home, I am theirs.

Chapter 7

Intimacy With God

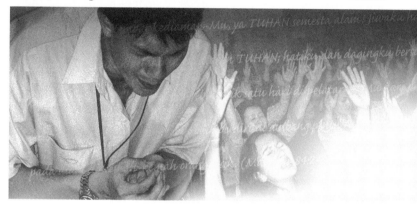

"He who dwells in the secret place of the Most High shall abide under the shadow of the Almighty" (Psalm 91:1 NKJV)

I HAVE often seen Pastor Philip cry because of the presence of God, though I know he is not a young man who easily sheds tears, especially considering his past.

I attended the opening of the Mawar Sharon Church in Jember, a city on the island of Java, nearly 100 miles southeast of Surabaya. Pastor Philip was weeping and broken. When he said the presence of God was very strong around the pulpit, I didn't believe it. Why only the pulpit? Did that mean the Lord only manifests His presence there?

But I didn't want to debate with him. I reminded myself that I was there only to report the grand opening of the Jember satellite church for the Mawar Sharon bulletin. I took out a pen and began to write, occasionally glancing toward the pulpit. I hoped that dozens, even hundreds of people would flock there. That would make a big story, one that would shake the heart of everyone who read it. I aimed the camera where he was kneeling, but people's hands were raised, obstructing my view. I decided to move forward to the front so I could see what was going on. But as soon as I sat down in the first row of chairs, the presence of God electrified me, and I began to weep.

I thought I was the only one crying, but when I stood up, I saw Samuel, the Jember pastor, kneeling with his hands open wide, and several others in the first row all weeping spontaneously because of the presence of God. Pastor Philip was right.

What was the secret to Pastor Philip's worship? Why had he found it difficult to submit to people in the past, but now he so readily submits to the Lord? What made a man who was once so hardened and easily provoked become tenderhearted and patient? I discovered the key to his transformation at a pastors' retreat.

A Light Mist

There was a retreat for the Mawar Sharon churches and the sister churches under Pastor Samuel Handoko's oversight. After dinner, Pastor Philip led the final session. He had planned to speak about vision. He began his sermon, then stopped. His eyes

Revival Service at PTC Supermall, 2004

filled with tears as he lifted his notes high so everyone in the auditorium could see them.

"Ladies, gentlemen, friends, I prepared a sermon about vision before this retreat. These are my sermon notes. But the Holy Spirit just told me clearly that I must speak instead about an intimate relationship with the Lord. I do not know why, but I must obey Him."

He began to speak about his walk with the Holy Spirit. I had heard his story before, but this time was different. I couldn't take my eyes off the pulpit area as I saw a light mist in two layers descending and ascending around him. It was as if the mist covered and protected him from something, though I do not know what. I had never seen anything like the mist before, but I knew by the Spirit that it was the anointing and presence of God.

Those concepts had been familiar to me since childhood. I am the daughter of a pastor, and missionaries from many nations, including Korea, Australia, Holland, and America used to visit my home. They would pray for hours with tears, but I had never seen a mist around them.

Why did the mist cover only him? Why didn't it swirl around the other pastors? And why was I the only one who saw it? Maybe I was exhausted from lack of sleep. I kept rubbing my eyes, but the light mist kept moving up and down where he stood, protecting and covering him. My heart was on fire. My eyes began to tear, and slowly, I started to cry. I ended up sitting on the floor weeping.

As Pastor Philip neared the end of his sermon about intimacy with the Lord, the mist filled almost the entire altar area. It had spread throughout the room, though primarily around the altar. I thought even he could not hold back tears with the presence of God covering him. A moment later he knelt and wept as if something were wounding him. Why was he crying like that?

Then all the people in the front rows approached and knelt before the altar, crying hard. Pastor Philip had not even invited them to come forward. All he did was to kneel and worship. I realized that it was the mist that drew the people to the altar. That night we celebrated the Holy Spirit. The Lord was our host, and I realized that the Lord had used Philip Mantofa to usher in His presence. Wherever he went, the Lord's presence was with him and His anointing covered him.

A few days after the retreat, I was in the computer room when Ongky Kusuma, the head of the multimedia ministry at Mawar Sharon Church, entered the room.

"Sianne, when did you see that mist?"

"Ongky, how did you know about that?"

"From Pastor Philip. I was with him when you sent him a text message about it. He held up his cell phone so I could read it. When did you see it, Sianne?"

"When Pastor Philip was preaching about intimacy with God."

"You didn't see it before that?"

I shook my head.

"What is it, Ongky?"

He smiled, "I'm not trying to fit my experience with what you saw, OK? But at that time, I had set up my video camera. It was ready and in focus. I didn't know why, but when I pointed the camera at Pastor Philip, the image became blurred, as if something was obstructing the lens. I thought my vision wasn't clear because of lack of sleep, so I rubbed my eyes and tried again. But I still couldn't see clearly. I tried to get a better image by angling the camera, but the result was the same, so I gave up. I shifted the lens to the retreat participants. I was surprised because the picture was sharp and clear. Then I went back and forth between Pastor Philip and the others to compare the image quality. The results surprised me. Every time I pointed the camera toward Pastor Philip, the image was cloudy. But when I shot footage of the retreat participants, it was bright and clear. Maybe your vision explains what actually happened."

The Burden of the Lord

One evening, about 200 intercessors gathered in the main hall for training and impartation. Pastor Philip opened the session, explaining the Word of God in simple terms so that even the new believers could easily understand. Knowing that too many believers tend to get caught up in the power of the anointing, he did not preach on power. Instead, his sermon focused on the beauty of an intimate relationship with the Lord. He was convinced that everyone who was intimate with the Lord and who befriended God would have a life and ministry filled with His anointing.

After his sermon, he invited every person present to stand arm in arm. Then he turned around, knelt by a corner of the pulpit, and began to worship and cry, weeping with great, choking sobs. He didn't say another word. The only sound that came out of his mouth was groaning.

It seemed to me that he was in deep conversation with the One he loved and was reluctant to leave Him to be with others. Perhaps for him, in that room there was only the Lord and him. I became impatient, wondering how long this meeting would go on if he stayed busy caught up with himself and the Lord. Didn't he know there were 201 people in that room (200 intercessors plus me) waiting for him to do something, like give a prophetic word, or lay hands on each one and pray? *He shouldn't be doing this here,* I thought to myself. But I was wrong.

As Pastor Philip worshiped and interceded *"with groanings which cannot be uttered"* (Rom. 8:26 NKJV), the Lord moved sovereignly and mightily. He touched everyone in that room. People were slain in the Spirit, laughing or crying out to God. All the while, Pastor Philip was kneeling in the same place. He didn't move from there. He only knelt and worshiped Him, and the Lord broke forth.

His Daily Bread

In 2004, I worked in Pastor Philip's office in order to write this book. I never once saw him fail to pray, even if it was only for half an hour before meeting with someone. He was like a machine that never stopped moving. In the midst of his busy schedule, he often would jog over to the sofa and began worshiping and speaking in tongues, calling softly on the name of the Lord.

I usually left the room at such times. For me, a person's quiet time with the Lord should be private. Just as it would be awkward to eavesdrop on an intimate conversation between a couple, when he began to cry and bring his complaints and petitions to the Lord, I stepped outside. Plus, I didn't want to interrupt him with the sound of typing on the computer keyboard. But after he saw me leave the room a few times, he insisted that I stay and continue working. After that, every time he prayed, I monitored him quietly. Sometimes he paced the floor while worshiping, and other times he sat and spoke in his spiritual language. But he almost always wept.

When Ongky entered his office one day, he noticed the guitar next to my typing desk.

"Whose guitar is that, Sianne?" he asked.

"Pastor Philip's guitar."

"What for?"

"When he prays, he plays that guitar."

"He has this, doesn't he?" he asked, pointing to the tape player. I shrugged my shoulders.

"Yes, but he expresses worships in his own way. He lives out the Word of God. When I was on a plane with him, the moment the passengers sat down, they began reading newspapers and magazines and eating and drinking. But Pastor Philip prayed in the Spirit and then read his Bible. He was not at all embarrassed to maintain his habit of worship in a public place."

According to Pastor Philip's mother and Maxi, when he was home he prayed for hours alone with the Lord in his room.

Pastor Peter Kaonang, overseer of the Mawar Sharon churches in Malang, Tulungagung, West Java, Jakarta, and Kalimantan, tried to duplicate the way he prayed, but he could not.

"I can imitate everything he does successfully—his ministry style, the way he motivates people, everything—except the one thing I always fail at—his all-night prayers. I am not that strong," he said, laughing.

I know that consistent prayer and Bible reading are Christian disciplines that need to be practiced. Pastor Philip can pray for hours without eating. In Canada, after he surrendered his life to the Lord, he would stay in his room to pray all day. At home, this habit sometimes worried his mother, who waited from morning until night for her second son to eat. When he didn't come downstairs, she knocked on his door and insisted that he eat something. Maxi once forced open the door to his room, impatient for his younger brother to come out. He had fallen asleep with the guitar in his hands.

"My brother is diligent in spending time with the Lord," Maxi said. "For him, prayer is like a daily meal. He won't skip it or miss it" (see John 4:31-34).

Because Pastor Philip constantly seeks the will of God and stays in communion with Him, he knows when to plan major events because he knows when God will move. It was evidently the Lord who directed him to make important plans for the summer of 2004.

Before the event, he isolated himself with Him. With his wife's blessing, he stayed alone in a church guest room, locked in for two days, to pray and read the Bible. From that room something awesome was born—the Festival of God's Power.

The Festival of God's Power

From the first day of the festival, the devil was defeated, sicknesses were healed, and hundreds of people confessed faith in

Christ. But what I sought, I found on the second day. When I entered the PTC Supermall, where the festival took place, God's presence was so strong it gripped the entire room. So I was not surprised when a lady from Malaysia with multiple sclerosis was instantly healed. She said that before the service even began, she saw Jesus enter the room and miraculously touch her.

That night, Pastor Philip preached about "The Invisible Hand."

"I want every person present to feel His tangible presence," he said. "When the presence of God is strong, those who are sick will not need to rely on their faith alone for God's power to touch them. His invisible hand is so close to the people that His presence will touch them where they hurt the most."

Pastor Philip at PTC Supermall

His faith moved God's heart. That day, everyone who was healed confessed to being touched by an invisible hand. A woman with crippled legs felt her legs pulled by someone invisible until finally, she stood upright. A paralyzed man said he felt something like fresh water flowing through him, and he could immediately jump up and stand. Another paralyzed woman who had to walk with a cane felt something hot touch her, and she could walk perfectly without her cane. Praise the Lord!

Pastor Philip had labored in the secret place of the Most High for the sake of seeing the Lord manifest His presence and touch the people. His presence was felt even more strongly when the worship team sang, "In the Presence of Jehovah." Everywhere people were weeping. Those were tears of joy because so many were healed and met their Savior that night. The service overflowed with faith, tears, and the power of God.

My Life Principles

My soul yearns, even faints, for the courts of the LORD; my heart and my flesh cry out for the living God. Even the sparrow has found a home, and the swallow a nest for herself, where she may have her young—a place near Your altar, O LORD Almighty, my King and my God....Better is one day in Your courts than a thousand elsewhere; I would rather be a doorkeeper in the house of my God than dwell in the tents of the wicked (Psalm 84:2-3,10).

Principle 1:
A Foundation of Love for the Lord

Many people build their ministry on the foundation of performance. I build my ministry on the foundation of love for the Lord. Whenever I feel the Lord sigh, even the gentlest sigh, I will leave a crowd to be alone with Him, even if it is only for five to ten seconds. The Lord knows my heart. He does not need to force me to fellowship with Him. He does not need to speak audibly to get me to kneel and pray. The Lord knows that my heart is always directed toward Him with love. At the gentlest flow of His power, without even asking, I immediately kneel.

Many people present something to the Lord, but how many give their gift without grumbling? Some present their lives to Him halfheartedly. Others give their lives to God out of fear of His judgment. But I give my whole heart to the Lord voluntarily so that He becomes the only person who satisfies my life. And the heart I give to Him is full of love.

Love, not power, is the greatest theme in my life. His love. That is why I am not surprised when someone misunderstands me and accuses me of being too emotional.

In Luke 7:38, the Lord Jesus was invited to eat with a Pharisee named Simon. A sinful woman entered the room and began to weep at Jesus' feet. She wet His feet with her tears, then wiped them with her hair. Apparently the Lord did not consider her worship as merely emotional behavior, although what that woman did obviously involved her emotions.

In fact, the Lord praised her and rebuked Simon: *"I came into your house. You did not give Me any water for My feet, but she wet My feet with her tears and wiped them with her hair"* (Luke 7:44). Without her awareness, the authors of the Gospels recorded what she had done. I believe what that woman did was inspired by the Holy Spirit. What the Lord Himself said of her, that *"wherever the gospel is preached throughout the world, what she has done will also be told, in memory of her"* (Mark 14:9), really happened. Even today, her works are remembered.

What was the difference between Jesus' relationship with Simon and with the woman? Both knew Him. Both met Jesus. But one of them not only knew the Lord, she loved Him deeply. That is the kind of love that I have in my heart for Him. It was a love that puzzled my friends in Vancouver.

In a Sunday service there, I worshiped the Lord wholeheartedly through songs. I felt the presence of God so strongly that I could not keep from crying. I knelt, though I did not see others kneel. On the way home from the service, a friend accused me of being overly emotional. Perhaps my kneeling and weeping were a reproach to him, just as King David's passionate worship offended his wife, Michal (see 2 Sam. 6:14-16).

I felt the real reason my friend rebuked me was not so much to criticize my enthusiasm, but to cover up his own spiritual deterioration. Yet I still considered him as my beloved brother.

Intimacy with the Lord does not always require words. Just by observing my body language, people are drawn to the presence of the Lord. Of course, those who refuse to draw close to the Lord feel uncomfortable or even convicted. They may resort to criticism so the emptiness of their hearts is not revealed.

I immediately challenged the friend who criticized me: "Ten years from now (it was then 1992) you will see that my love for the Lord will not have changed because His love for me will never change." I said that, not because I believed in myself, but because I trusted in God's love for me. Now more than ten years have passed, and I have successfully proved to my friends in Vancouver that my relationship with the Lord is not founded on mere emotions.

My life offends some people because they see in it a deep love for the Lord. Let people judge me. As long as what I do pleases the Lord, I do not care what others think of me. Because Jesus was pleased with the outpouring of that sinful woman's love, He chose to use her to glorify Himself—no matter what others thought of her. I envy her for one reason—her hair. If only I had long hair, I could wash the Lord's feet with it.

Principle 2:
Intimacy With a Whole Heart

No theory can teach you how to build an intimate relationship with the Lord, nor does any one way apply to all. Yet building intimacy with the Lord must develop out of yearning to be one with Him and close to Him. Although it may strike some as emotional, we cannot speak about intimacy with the Lord if we do not involve our innermost feelings. Intimacy with Him speaks about a whole heart. It is from the heart that we speak and feel. As Jesus said, *"...Out of the overflow of the heart the mouth speaks"* (Matt. 12:34).

Ever since I was saved and repented in 1992, I have sought after the Lord sincerely, and I began to build a personal relationship with Him. I did not look for a formula or learn from anyone else. Like King David's song in Psalm 63:8, *"My soul followeth hard after Thee..."* (ASV), my heart sought the Lord. Now our closeness cannot be expressed with words. It is not limited by space or time.

Once in the middle of a crowd, my mind withdrew and a deep thirst for the Lord overwhelmed my soul. All I desired to say was, "Lord, how I love You." I left everything and everyone behind just to express my heart to Him with that one statement.

Closeness with the Lord involves all my emotions. If God is hurt, I also feel hurt. If He is distanced from someone, I feel sad. If the Holy Spirit is misunderstood, I feel wounded. If He is grieved, I grieve. If He is happy, I rejoice in the Spirit. In intimacy with the Lord, we become one with Him, so identified with Him that His feelings become our own. My best times with the Lord take place past bedtime. At night I have fewer interruptions and competition for my time with Him. When the people I love are sound asleep, I go to the sofa in my bedroom. I sit there and spend quality time with the Lord. Usually, I am silent. Occasionally, I pray in tongues and say a few words, such as, "Lord, I need You." It's almost like dating the Lord. Some of my richest times with Him are spent in solitude.

Principle 3:
Prioritize Time With Him

Building an intimate and serious relationship with the Lord is so important that I would not exchange five minutes of my time with Him for five hours of power flowing through me in which people are resurrected from the dead. Actually, I would choose both if I could. But if I had to choose between time with Him and time accomplishing His mighty works, I would choose five minutes with the One I love. However, I believe that God will use those who are intimate with Him in extraordinary ways, and that will include the dead being raised through His life.

Principle 4:
The Christian Disciplines

We must determine a time and place to discipline our flesh through consistent prayer in the Spirit and Bible study. Spiritual discipline is not legalism—it is meant to be a blessing. If we don't have such discipline, we tend to be lazy and forget. In our flesh, we human beings make excuses, especially when we're busy. I have committed to communicate with the Lord in tongues for about 40 minutes a day.

Reading the Bible is also a must, for at least 40 minutes a day. I cover many chapters in the Bible every day. My goal is to put my flesh under control (see 1 Cor. 9:25-27). "Flesh, you are subject to the Spirit. Flesh, I am giving you a rule you must follow." But I make sure that the rule is imposed only on my flesh, not on my heart. My heart must always be free to express my love for Him any time and any place.

As I get busier, with many urgent tasks to be done, I have less privacy. But I still try to steal time alone with the Lord. Those sweet times usually come only after everyone is asleep. Then I can speak heart to heart with Him.

The benefits I derive from even five sweet minutes with the Lord may surpass the five-hour prayers of those who approach God legalistically. Unlike my daily disciplines of praying in tongues and Bible reading, I don't need 40 minutes to approach the presence of God. Five minutes is enough, provided it is quality time. Of course, I don't try to limit this time to five minutes.

Being in the Lord's presence not only provides me with intimacy with Him—it also builds my faith and develops my spiritual man.

Principle 5:
The Lord's Usher

In the Old Testament, the Lord did not allow just anyone to carry the ark of His presence. Only the priests who wore special robes could usher in the presence of God in this way. Though God was omnipresent throughout the Israelite camp, it was the priests who brought the congregation deeper into the presence of God. In the New Testament, the veil in the temple was torn in two when Jesus died on the cross (see Matt. 27:51). This was a sign that the way had been made clear for all who accept Jesus Christ to enter into the presence of God (see Heb. 6:19-20; 9:24). While His presence is available today to all of His children because of the atonement, some are chosen and supernaturally gifted to bring the Lord's congregation into a deeper dimension of His presence.

I am not a gifted singer, but if the Lord leads me to sing in the middle of a sermon, the entire atmosphere changes and people's faces reflect the strong presence of God. I did not understand at first why this happened, so I asked the Lord about it. His answer was beyond my expectations.

"Philip, I have designated you to lead my congregation into My presence. That is your principal task."

Once the Lord revealed this to me, I learned not to worry about my performance or my appearance in the pulpit or on the platform. My only job is to lead the congregation into the presence of the Lord. I am just the Lord's usher, one who wears a priestly robe with a unique anointing—to usher His people into the throne room of grace where they can be touched by God (see Exod. 28:2,41).

Testing the Heart

The Lord used me for a season to heal many who were sick. I just knocked on someone's door and the sick person was instantly healed. In the following weeks, incredible healings occurred. I thought the Lord had set me aside for the healing ministry. But then one day, He gave me a vision.

I saw an older man sitting in a rocking chair. The man had many fields. He ordered one of His servants to call me. I was in a rice field, working with sophisticated tools. When I found Him, I knelt before Him, beside His chair.

"What is it, Father?" I asked.

"Philip, hand over all your tasks in that field to others." He told me.

I was shocked. "Father, I am at the peak of my success," I protested. "Miracles are taking place."

"I know. I have other servants who will continue the work."

The Lord had called me to His feet to ask me to return the tools of His power of healing, which He Himself had given to me. I was surprised.

"Then what work will I do?"

"You will be here, close to me, pleasing my heart."

It was not easy to release that ministry. By then, the ministry of healing had captivated my heart. I really had to struggle to give it all up to Him.

I finally understood that the mantle of His anointing for any ministry was only by grace. I did not have the right to hold onto it. But I had come to enjoy the power so much that it was difficult for me to surrender it back to its Owner. Nevertheless, this was the Lord's request. He wanted me only to be in His presence. Finally, after a struggle, I surrendered.

"Yes, Father. I will surrender all my tools to You."

I spoke like that because I thought it was only a test of obedience, like Abraham, who surrendered his only son Isaac to the Lord, but then received him back again (see Gen. 22:1-18). But the Lord really did take that ministry away from me. From that moment on, it was as if that grace had been removed from me.

My ministry was not as spectacular for a few years. But during that time, God gave me many new songs that spoke to my heart. I did not have the gift of healing any longer. I could knock on the door until it broke down and no one would get healed.

One of the songs I wrote in those days is below:

> *My heavenly Father, only You I praise*
> *I know I'm not alone again*
> *My heavenly Father, thank You for Your love and care*
> *I feel the peace and warmth of Your hand.*
> *I'm not alone again, not alone again*
> *Father is with me wherever I am*
> *I love You, Father, I love You, Father*
> *I love You, Father, my King*

The songs came forth in the presence of the Father. When I surrendered the mantle of healing, the Father exchanged it for the mantle of His presence. From that moment on, whenever I worship, the presence of the Father immediately falls upon me.

A prophet once said of the spiritual robe I wear, "You have been given a different robe than your friends, one that enables you to minister in the Father's throne room, and you are able to immediately enter in. Therefore, go, and bring the people into the deep presence of God."

That robe continues to be the heart of my ministry. Whenever I pray, the fragrance of Christ starts pouring forth (see Song of Sol. 1:3; 2 Cor. 2:14-15). His presence comes until I stop praying. This mantle the Father has given me to wear brings down the presence of God. And there is nothing I love more than His presence.

Chapter 8

Mantle of Power

THE three most outstanding characteristics of the Lord's work in Pastor Philip's life are his intimacy with the Lord, the continual transformation of his character, and a faith that expects great things. But sometimes his faith puzzled me.

He scheduled a revival service for April 2003 and asked me to write an article for the church bulletin called "The Song of Deborah," based on Judges 5. By faith he made plans to invite a living witness whose testimony at the service was to be the subject of the article. He was asking me to write an article in advance about someone we didn't know yet. I was dubious about his publication strategy.

"Take home my Bible and make a copy of God's promises for this revival service," he told me. "Four weeks before the revival, publish it in the bulletin. Write it both as an article and in advertisement format. Write it to inspire people to become a blessing to their peers and to bring their friends to the service. Two weeks before the revival, our bulletin should feature the testimony of someone healed by the Lord. If this is difficult, ask the pastors to help you find someone." Then he handed me the Bible, full of notes in his handwriting.

Copying the notes in his Bible and promoting the event in the bulletin were simple enough. Writing an article that would stir the enthusiasm of the congregation to invite unbelieving friends was not difficult either. But where would I find a living witness?

Despite my doubts, I followed his plan. Time passed. He called me again and encouraged me that the revival service would reap a great victory. To affirm his faith in the Lord's promise, he chose the theme, "Empty out Hell, Populate Heaven."

Then he reiterated, "By two weeks before the revival, you should have found a new believer whose life was recently turned around by God. Include that person's testimony in the bulletin. He or she will be the living witness we need to help renew the congregation's faith."

Living witness? The words went around in my head continuously. I didn't know how to find that person. Where should I look?

In March, "The Song of Deborah" was published in the bulletin, in the form of a summons to wage war against the devil.

Posters announcing the revival service were plastered everywhere. All of us were busy with preparations. I was drowning in other work and forgot all about the plan to find a living witness. As the time approached to publish the witness's testimony, I still hadn't found anyone. Panic made it difficult for me to sleep. I was troubled. But when I surrendered, the Lord sent me a surprise.

One week before the deadline, I found a letter on my desk which Pastor Philip had forwarded to me. I ripped open the envelope and read it excitedly.

"On March 8, 2003, without any warning, I started coughing up blood from my mouth and nose. I had not felt sick before that. I panicked, but there was nothing I could do except become resigned to my fate. A family friend came over and offered to pray for me. I realized that her offer to pray meant that she was a Christian. This conflicted with my religious beliefs, but my desire to be healed was greater. So I decided to accept Jesus and surrendered my illness to Him. When our friend prayed for me, nothing miraculous happened. Even so, I went to her church a few days later, hoping to be healed. I held out until the church meeting was over, but I was still sick.

"As I left the sanctuary and got into the elevator, I started coughing until I vomited blood. Immediately my mother and I returned to the sanctuary. We approached Pastor Philip Mantofa and asked him to pray for me. He only prayed for a moment, but that day I was healed. The coughing and vomiting of blood completely stopped. My condition is continuing to improve and the sickness never returned. From that moment, I was sure that I made the right choice. The next day I surrendered my life completely to Jesus, and was baptized by Pastor Jonathan Abdul Madjid. Now I feel like a different person than I was before."

As I read the letter, I was so stunned that I screamed out loud, "I found you. Finally, I found you!" I didn't know whether to laugh or cry. Without realizing it, I attained to a new level of faith with that letter in my hand, even though it was a tiny mustard seed. This woman was the living witness whom God had prepared and Pastor Philip had been expectantly believing and waiting for.

In April 2003, the long-awaited revival service at Kertajaya Sports Stadium finally arrived. On the first day, dozens of people were miraculously healed, 932 souls received Jesus, and 225 people were baptized. On the second day, 148 people were baptized, dozens were healed, and hundreds more received the infilling of the Holy Spirit and the gift of tongues. The Lord had used one man's faith to birth this revival and to inspire and to multiply the faith of others—including mine.

Pastor Philip's strategy for that revival service was proof to me of his faith to see the invisible (see Heb. 11:27). In his daily journal, I found a statement of faith that inspired the growth of my own: "Thinking about great things will push us to make great plans that in the end will produce great results."

That year, 600 children filled the church at a children's revival service. As Pastor Philip preached, nearly 550 children ran to the altar crying. Almost 100 were baptized that night. Many amazing phenomena escaped notice of the camera or human eyes.

A nanny accompanying her charge, who understood neither the anointing nor the presence of God was touched by the Holy Spirit.

Beneath the church stairs, tables had been set up for registration. The nanny had joined the line of hundreds of children to register Josephine, her employer's daughter. Although she did not yet know Jesus, she cried the entire time that she waited in line. The power of God was stirring her heart, and the harder she tried to stop crying, the more tears she shed. When the Word of God was proclaimed, she felt called to accept Jesus as her Lord and Savior. Unembarrassed to be the sole adult among a throng of children, she went forward and confessed her faith in Jesus for the first time. She was baptized that same night. She later said she felt God's presence as soon as she entered the church yard.

The Mawar Sharon Church in Surabaya grew rapidly. By 2004, the congregation reached more than 30,000 members and

Children's Revival Service, 2003

70 local churches. Pastor Philip preached that faith should not easily surrender or look to circumstances. He encouraged the people to trust in God's power, not looking at their limitations. Miracles happened among those who believed this message. One of them was Mrs. Siu Cien.

Siu Cien's Testimony

"In 1998 I often experienced hemorrhaging. I was diagnosed with a myoma, a small benign tumor, in my uterus. My doctor told me that surgery was the only way to remove it. Although the tumor was not life-threatening, I suffered from excruciating pain during menstruation.

"In March 2002, as Pastor Philip Mantofa preached the Word of the Lord, he declared that the Lord would heal the sick that night. I immediately believed. To my amazement, he then announced that the Lord had just healed a woman's uterus. At that moment, the Lord touched me so that my entire body trembled. I was certain that He had healed my uterus.

"A few months later, I returned to my doctor. He could not find the myoma during the ultrasound. The Lord had removed it! I no longer feel pain during my monthly cycle. Praise the Lord!

"I experienced a second miracle at Mawar Sharon in May 2002. I had had severe headaches since 1995, sometimes accompanied by convulsions. I even passed out once. That afternoon Pastor Philip was preaching. He declared the Lord would come and meet His congregation's needs. I immediately prayed to the Lord, asking for healing. Suddenly I felt a flow of electricity touching my head and coursing through my entire body. I knew I was healed. I never had a headache again."

Faith at Work

Because of this woman's faith she received not one, but two miracles. This was a living lesson for me, for I had not understood that faith could be imparted. Every time I saw a miracle, I thought it was due to the sovereignty of God. I did not comprehend how the Lord co-labors through the faith of a man or woman of God who is praying for the sick or needy. Nor did I realize the way He responds to those who reach out to Him in faith (see Mark 5:34). My eyes were opened even more during the Festival of God's Power in June 2004 at the PTC Supermall.

On the second day of the festival, I chose a seat in the fifth row directly in front of the stage where I could watch every detail of the event. From the beginning of the service, I had a heightened sense of expectancy. My heart was pounding.

God answered the cry of my heart. In the midst of the glorious healing testimonies, something happened that taught me a lesson and quickened my faith. Thank God. Not by coincidence, I received the experience by observing three people who wanted to see a demonstration of God's power.

I sat beside a woman who attended with her husband and a friend. Seeing her astonishment as events unfolded, I realized that she was not from our church. A polite conversation revealed that she was visiting from church to church. Without realizing it, the woman beside me inspired me to believe that God can use anyone who is willing.

"The preacher must be from outside the country, right?" she asked me.

"No, ma'am. The preacher is from Surabaya," I answered with a smile.

"Oh, really? Is he from Mawar Sharon Church? He seems young to be a pastor."

When I pointed out several other pastors from our church who passed by, she was increasingly surprised.

"Wow, they are all still young, aren't they?"

"Yes, they are."

"That is amazing," she said. "Usually when churches hold major events, they invite a famous preacher from overseas to draw a crowd. The local pastors usually only coordinate and host the event. But everyone here is from Mawar Sharon?"

She did not wait for my reply, but turned toward her husband and whispered.

"The preacher is from Mawar Sharon."

Her husband lifted his eyebrows in surprise. As the testimonies of miracles poured forth from the stage, these three people enthusiastically clapped their hands.

"Look, the lame are walking! The lame are walking!"

"Wow, look, he was healed! Isn't that amazing?"

As I observed their reactions, I realized that they did not come to the festival to meet with the Lord or to be healed, but to watch the Lord demonstrate His power. Apparently, there was nothing wrong with that. After a paralyzed man walked and climbed up to the stage to testify, Pastor Philip shouted to the counselors at the foot of the platform, "Where is his wheelchair? Bring the wheelchair here and put it on the stage. Let the devil be ashamed when he sees it."

His words of faith stunned me, and the woman beside me stood and clapped her hands, shouting, "Wow. This is the first time I have ever heard anyone bold enough to say that!"

My heart was on fire. After that night, I believed their lives would never be the same. They had finally found a faith that could be an example for them in their search.

Those two days of the Festival of God's Power were filled with miracles—hernias, uterine cancer, paralysis, blindness, deafness, hemorrhoids, sinusitis, asthma, stroke, and other diseases were miraculously healed. Many of those healed were not believers in Christ. From a young child who suffered from a heart anomaly to a 100-year-old grandmother who could not walk, the Lord healed people while they were sitting in their seats.

Even several hours before the festival began, the Lord touched and healed many people. The presence of God was so strong in that place. It was like a mantle of power that covered the building. People who came in confessed that God's presence was so pervasive it could be felt outside the building. Others claimed to be healed as the songs of praise were lifted.

That night people went to the stage to testify how the Lord had healed them. It was not only a day of liberation from their sicknesses, but also the beginning of their faith. Praise the Lord!

After the festival was over, testimonies continued to pour in. One was that of Rosita.

Rosita's Testimony

"My younger sister became ill in July 2003. Suddenly, her hemoglobin count dropped, and she became feverish and weak. She was already taking medication prescribed by three doctors in Malang but to no avail. The doctors gave up. Before I went to Surabaya for the festival, we had her checked at a laboratory. The lab results indicated an anomaly in her blood, but the doctor could not provide an accurate diagnosis. We took her to the larger city of Surabaya, but doctors there prescribed only vitamins. They did not give her a blood transfusion or medications. Based on her symptoms, the doctor suspected she had lupus.

"One week before the Festival of God's Power, I went home to Malang. I was surprised to see that her face was yellow. She seemed deathly pale. I recommended a blood test to find out if her hemoglobin had decreased again. On June 1, 2004, her hemoglobin was 8. (The normal range for women is 12 to 15.5.) But I was not worried because it was not the first time her blood work had tested at that level. On June 4, before I returned to Surabaya, I felt there was something strange about her deteriorating condition so I insisted she be checked again at the laboratory. My suspicions were confirmed. Her hemoglobin had dropped drastically and was now 5. By June 8, her hemoglobin had fallen to 4.

"That was the first day of the Festival of God's Power. I invited her to come with me, but she refused, saying her condition made it impossible for her to travel. The next day her hemoglobin was 4.4. I left for Surabaya, but was so worried about her condition that I made plans to return to Malang that evening. Then a friend from Mawar Sharon Church encouraged me to come to the festival.

"I sent my sister a text message from the service. 'I am at a healing crusade. I know you are far away, but please join in faith with me here. Ask your husband not to admit any visitors for now. I'll keep in touch via text messages.'

"From the moment the praise began, through Pastor Philip's preaching the Word of the Lord, I sent her a steady barrage of text messages, including everything Pastor Philip said, word for word. When he declared, 'It doesn't depend on me. I don't need to touch you, for that's not the answer. This is the answer: As I release what comes from the Lord and as you receive it, you will be healed.'

"I sent those words to her immediately. When Pastor Philip prayed, I did not close my eyes because I had to send every single word of his prayer to her. Slowly but surely, my faith began to rise.

"'Whoever is beside you, ask him or her to agree with you in prayer.' Pastor Philip said. I wrote it and joined in prayer.

"'Now, I release healing to those who are sick.'

"I caught his words of faith and passed them on to my sister. After the prayer was over, I was convinced my sister had been healed. Even though she was not at the festival, I believed the

Lord had given her a long-distance miracle (see Matt. 8:5-13). My faith was immediately tested by a relative who had also come at the festival. He offered to help me get my sister to Singapore for medical attention.

"He was not the only one who had suggested medical treatment outside the country. Everyone who knew my sister's condition recommended we take her to Singapore or China, where medical facilities were more sophisticated. But I was certain she was already healed.

"Then a man went forward and testified how his mother at home had been healed. He had prayed and had faith for his mother to be able to move her body again. When he called home, his wife informed him that his mother had risen from her sick bed. When my friends heard that story, they asked me to call my sister to be certain. But I refused because I believed she was already healed. Besides, her healing had to be medically verified by a blood test. So there was no reason to telephone her.

"By the next day, the miracle was evident. Her hemoglobin had climbed from 4.4 to 5.2. When they checked her again on Friday, her hemoglobin count was 8. The doctor had not given her any medication. As her condition improved, the doctor promised she could go home earlier than he had estimated. 'I will give you two more weeks. If in two weeks your hemoglobin level is 12, you can go home.'

"I tried to encourage her. 'Just believe that on Tuesday you will be home. Get checked again on Monday.'

"On Monday her hemoglobin had climbed to 12.1. The doctor was amazed. 'What have you been eating?' he asked.

"I know it was the hand of the Lord. If the doctor had given my sister medicine, maybe we wouldn't have called it a miracle. But he had given her nothing—no medications, transfusions, or proper treatment. In light of her deteriorating condition, I had lodged a strong protest with the doctor. So when she was healed without any medical intervention, we knew it was the Lord. The DNA test had confirmed that my sister had lupus—but not anymore. The Lord set her free."

My Life Principles

Principle:
Pass on Your Mantle

> *For the kingdom of God is not a matter of talk but of power* (1 Corinthians 4:20).

We read about a mantle of anointing in the story of the prophets, Elijah and Elisha. When Elisha joined Elijah as his disciple, he saw what Elijah accomplished through that mantle. When there was no boat or other means to cross the Jordan, Elijah struck the water with his mantle and the river parted (see 2 Kings 2:8). After they arrived on the other side, the waters of the river Jordan returned to their normal courses.

When Elijah was caught up to Heaven in a chariot of fire, Elisha was perplexed. How could he return to the other side? Elijah was no longer there. Now who could help him? He alone remained with Elijah's mantle, which had been dropped not far from where he was standing. When Elisha saw Elijah's unclaimed mantle, he took it and put it on, though not literally. For he rolled up the mantle saying, "Where is the God of Elijah?" Then he struck the edge of the river Jordan with it. He did exactly what Elijah had done earlier. Miraculously, the river immediately parted, and Elisha crossed over (see 2 Kings 2:14).

Thus the power of a man of God mightily used by the Lord was transferred to his disciple. The mantle is a symbol of God's power. Before Elijah was caught up to Heaven by the Lord, he transferred his mantle to Elisha. It is a shame that Elisha did not do the same. He wore his mantle to the grave, where his bones raised a dead man to life. This was his final miracle (see 2 Kings 13:21). If Elisha had transferred his mantle during his lifetime, could God have resurrected a generation of the Lord's army who in turn could have revived many dead? Only God knows.I also have a mantle in ministry given to me by the Lord. It is my mantle of God's power. I am determined to walk in the power of the Holy Spirit—and transferring that power has become a trademark of my ministry. I made a solemn promise to the Lord.

"Lord, I do not want to be like pastors from previous generations. They transfer the mantle of their ministry to others when they are on their deathbeds. I will transfer my mantle to others during my lifetime, while I am still actively being used by You in the power of the Holy Spirit. I do not want to repeat Elisha's mistake."

Since the day I made that vow, I always impart what I receive from the Lord to my spiritual children. I will not keep it for myself. I will not carry that power to the grave. The power has been given for the sake of the Gospel.

Evangelism must not stop when a man of God dies, but must continue until this world is filled with God's glory. So why keep the means of walking in God's anointing a secret? I see many pastors and preachers whose ministry and anointing are outstanding, but others just see the work. That is because they do not reveal their secrets. They leave it to the authors of their biographies—if they have any—to guess the secret of their power after they die.

Let us not become like that. Let us follow the example of Christ, who at the outset of His ministry prayed and chose 12 disciples who later continued it. He taught them everything He knew. Usually a person chooses a successor just before he dies or when his ministry is almost at an end. But our Lord Jesus was different.

He gave His disciples power from the beginning of His ministry (see Mark 3:13-15). He gave them a chance. That principle of Jesus Christ has become my principle today. I am convinced that anyone can be used by God as an extension of His hand. Because power is not an end in itself, the true purpose of wearing the mantle is to glorify God and co-labor with Him to change and transform human lives. It is also essential to bear in mind that the daily renewal of our character as He conforms us to His holiness is as important as the mantle.

I do not want the Lord to use me alone. I hope God will also use my spiritual children even more than me. As long as He uses me, others are welcome to learn from my life. I know God never uses people in the same way, but at least my disciples will have an example in me to push them to find their own mantles of anointing. That is my principle and the reason this book was written.

**"I will never remember your sins
because I am your father."**

Chapter 9

Spiritual Fatherhood

"I write to you, fathers, because you have known Him who is from the beginning" (1 John 2:13a).

"**W**HETHER a child is my own flesh and blood, adopted, or a spiritual child, they are all my children and they will be treated the same," Pastor Philip said. "Whether they go to Mawar Sharon or not, all of them are my beloved children in the faith."

It is not denomination or church affiliation that bonds the churches founded by Pastor Philip's disciples with Mawar Sharon. Rather, it is the love relationship between a spiritual father and his spiritual children. Distance cannot separate them, nor can they be removed from the heart and the mind (see Isa. 49:16).

During a frenetic week of back-to-back revival services at school campuses in Manado, the capital of North Sulawesi Province, Pastor Yosef Moro Wijaya, the pastor of Mawar Sharon in Sumatra, shared a room with Pastor Philip. As we spoke, it was evident that he valued Pastor Philip not only as an older brother in the Lord, but also as a leader and spiritual father.

"It was rainy season in Manado and the roads were muddy," he said. "On the third day, I noticed his shoes were covered in mud. He seemed exhausted and desperately in need of rest. So I quietly took his shoes and began cleaning them."

"What did you use to clean the shoes, Pastor Moro?" I asked.

"First I tried a tissue. But eventually I had to use my fingers."

"Your fingers?" I asked, surprised.

"The tissue got mushy when it got wet, and it couldn't clean in the cracks, so I had to use my fingernails."

Pastor Moro's Story

"One of the ministries Pastor Philip instructed me in was deliverance. In the beginning, it took him hours to cast out demons. But he patiently endured until the demons were gone. As his ministry grew in the Lord's power and authority, at just the mention of the name of Jesus, the devils fled.

"He taught me the key to casting out satan. 'Moro, you must know one thing. In the ministry of deliverance, you are the one who has the authority, not the devil' (see Matt. 28:18; Luke 9:1).

Early ministry in Ungaran, 1994

"'Never ask a demon to leave. Exert the authority the Lord Jesus has given you. Crush his mentality, but do not allow him to crush yours. Speak loudly so the devil knows you're not afraid of him.'

"One day Pastor Philip invited me to his room to see a demonstration up close. 'Moro, sit here and watch me pray. You don't need to say, "Amen" or do anything at all. Just observe.'

"I sat leaning against the door, as he prayed, kneeling beside his bed. He sang and worshiped the Lord for more than an hour while plucking his guitar. Squatting by the door, I waited and watched. He stayed in that position for a long time.

"Of his many prayers that day, what I remember most is, 'Lord, You are very precious. Do not separate me from Your love. You are more than everything. Lord, I love You.' Then I heard my name mentioned as he prayed for me. From that day on, I have modeled his quiet time.

"Discipleship for him means sharing his values and lifestyle. Since he lives what he teaches, he disciples not with a theory, but by demonstrating a living Word. To inspire love for God's Word, he loans his Bible to his disciples. 'As you read this Bible, observe how I meditate on the Word of the Lord every day and take notes in my Bible,' he said.

"As I learned from the example of his life, my own method of discipling became similar to his. I now teach people what I have learned myself. I have even invited people to my prayer room to teach them how to pray and read the Word. 'Sit here, watch and learn,' I tell them."

A Father Who Is Always There

"Pastor Philip stays in touch with me and is always available when I need his advice. If he's in a meeting, he always returns my frequent, long-distance calls from his cell phone. He lives out his belief that a father is the giver, not only of his resources, but of his time as well. Sometimes we talk for 20 minutes to an hour or more, and not just about ministry. He also shares recent experiences and new principles the Lord has taught him. He asks about members he knows from the church that I pastor. He cares about their spiritual walks and often explains the best ways to follow up with new believers.

"When I go to Surabaya, I usually stay at his house. His fathering is demonstrated in simple ways—it's not limited to church meetings or discipleship classes. As he flows in the natural circumstances of daily life, he takes those opportunities to impart his life values and teachings to me.

"When a long time elapsed between our meetings, I felt spiritually dry, so he asked me to visit him in Surabaya from time to time. But I couldn't always afford the trips. He knew this, so he gave me money.

"'Moro, do you have enough money?' he asked.

"'No, Pastor Philip, I have no more money,' I replied.

"As my spiritual father, he wanted to teach me that a father must learn to give sacrificially. In Surabaya, he even invited me to my favorite restaurant to eat dim sum. He always treated me as a special guest. Though I didn't consider myself worthy of that treatment, his behavior made me feel special in his eyes. Through his love and nurturing, I grew in the Lord."

Love Is Tested

"No one can deny the relationship between a father and his child. No matter what happens, their relationship is based, not on the child's achievements, behavior, or perfect grades, but because he is his father's flesh and blood. It is like that for me spiritually. Pastor Philip accepted me, not because I am important or talented, but because I am his spiritual son.

"One day I fell into sin. Pastor Philip traveled to Ungaran especially to meet with me. That day I received many harsh reprimands from him. On the one hand, I saw the anger of a father, and on the other, I saw the compassionate love of a father who accepted me as I was. Crushed in my spirit, I wept in remorse because I knew I was wrong. But when I acknowledged my sin, Pastor Philip threw his arms around me and prayed for me.

"Afterward, I was sanctioned and forbidden to participate in pulpit ministry for six months. It was a painful process, but I accepted the decision in quiet obedience and trust. My commitment to sit in the front row of my church during services embarrassed me because many people asked why I wasn't in charge. I didn't answer them. Even that difficult experience helped me understand fatherhood.

"Many people, including me, did not comprehend the significance of Pastor Philip's spiritual fatherhood in my life. One day, Pastor Samuel Handoko and I went to Surabaya to discuss the churches in Salatiga and Ungaran with Pastor Philip. When we arrived at his house, Pastor Philip and Irene were not home. While waiting for their return, we talked with Pastor Jusuf Soetanto, Pastor Philip's father-in-law and the senior pastor of Mawar Sharon Church. When Pastor Philip returned, I was so happy I wanted to smile. Instead, I cried.

"Pastor Philip invited us into the dining room, where Pastor Samuel spoke about Pastor Philip's apostleship over his churches. When he had finished, Pastor Samuel excused himself and went to rest. Once I was alone with Pastor Philip, I said, 'Pastor, I do not understand the bond between you and me, but the moment I saw you, I felt so happy that I started to cry.'

"I realized through that inexplicably great joy how precious our relationship had become for my walk and discipleship before the Lord. After that, I promised to meet with him as often as possible.

"My submission to my spiritual fathers outweighs my submission to my family because, from the beginning, I knew Pastor Philip was tracking my spiritual growth and praying for me continually. Although he can never replace my family or their role in my life, as the one who raised me up in Christ, Pastor Philip fulfills a unique role as a spiritual father.

"Most people know Pastor Philip as an anointed man of God. But not everyone knows the ordinary man behind the anointing. He also plays basketball and shares stories and laughs with us. When he is tired, I give him a massage or walk on his back. During such relaxing moments, we discuss light topics and just have a good time hanging out together.

"But when it comes to significant issues, I submit to his and Pastor Samuel's advice out of deep respect for the investment they have made in my life. I obey for two reasons. First, I believe they see things in me that I cannot. Second, I want to please them, like Gideon's troops who shouted, 'A sword for the LORD and for Gideon' (Judg. 7:20b)."

"Moro," I asked, "If the Lord started to use you more than Pastor Philip, would you forget him and leave him behind?"

"Never," he answered. "He is a part of my life. He is not just a teacher, but a father to me. When students graduate, they leave their teachers behind. At one of Pastor Philip's discipleship sessions in Surabaya, some people prayed to have his anointing. I don't feel comfortable with that kind of prayer. So I asked the Lord to mature me quickly so I could help carry the burden that Pastor Philip bears. I want to consider his needs, not just my own."

Pastor Judy Koesmanto's Testimony

Another young leader Pastor Philip influenced was Pastor Judy Koesmanto, a man of God who is district pastor for Mawar Sharon churches in Surabaya.

"Mawar Sharon Senior Pastor Jusuf Soetanto was in Canada when he heard about the church split and that people were leaving the church. The first person he asked about was me. 'Is Judy leaving?'

"Rumors had it that every prominent church leader was on the way out, including me. So without pausing to think, the news bearer answered, 'Yes, even Judy is leaving.'

"Pastor Jusuf rejected the rumor resolutely. 'Impossible. I know him. I know he is not leaving like the others.'

"He said that without knowing where I stood, perhaps because of the bond between a spiritual father and his son. But the truth is, the leaders and I had planned our mass exodus from the church without Pastor Jusuf's knowledge. We had conspired to all leave together on August 16, 2000. But Pastor Jusuf discovered our plan prematurely on July 15. So we moved the plan up and decided to leave immediately, on Sunday, July 16.

"That year, Pastor Philip was a newcomer to Mawar Sharon. Before this incident, he had never asked anything of me, since I had more pastoral authority than him at that time. In fact, we seldom communicated. So I was caught by surprise when he unexpectedly called.

"'Brother Judy, are you able to come over to my house right now?'

"For some reason, I couldn't refuse. I went to his house. As he spoke, my heart became softer and I grew increasingly uneasy. 'Brother Judy, I don't know if you are friend or foe. But I am moved by the Lord to speak with you about this situation,' he said.

"'Philip, from the beginning, I know what I did was wrong,' I found myself confessing. 'I have actually decided not to leave the church, even though it may be too late. I am ready to face any consequences and to take the risk. Philip, I am a sinful man. I am prepared for this church to reject me and never to use me again. But, I will certainly stay. Even if all my positions are removed and I am fired from full-time ministry, I will remain faithful to this church.'

"I don't know why I spoke so boldly. Pastor Philip encouraged me. 'I trust you, brother Judy. Although a few hours ago you were on the opposing side, I still trust you.'

"That's what finally broke my heart. All the negative thoughts about the church leadership that had been planted and taken root in my heart years before were instantly destroyed. At that moment, I made the decision to live under authority. 'Pastor Philip, starting today I will submit to you. I surrender to your leadership over my life and future. I will obey and follow you, as you follow Christ.'

"I could scarcely believe my own response. Certainly, Pastor Philip's words revived my heart and enabled me to speak boldly with faith. For sure, it was by faith because I didn't even know him very well. But I sensed he could be trusted.

"The next day I met with Senior Pastor Jusuf at the Westin Hotel. At first, I didn't have the courage to meet with him because I was embarrassed and ashamed. I felt like a traitor and a rebel, and I couldn't see beyond my guilt. With my steps dragging, I entered the room where Pastor Jusuf was waiting. The moment he saw me, he embraced me, weeping.

"'Judy, I am your father. No matter how wrong you are, I will never remember your sins because I am your father.'

"His words broke my heart and demolished every negative thought and attitude I had harbored toward him. I felt like Peter when Jesus asked,

> *"Do you truly love* [agape—divine, unconditional love and spiritual devotion] *Me more than these?" "Yes, Lord,"* *he said, "You know that I love* [phileo—the affection of close friendship] *You." ...Again Jesus said, "Simon son of John, do you truly love* [agape] *Me?" He answered,* *"Yes, Lord, You know that I love* [phileo] *You. "...The*

*third time He said to him, "Simon son of John, do you
love [phileo] Me?" Peter was hurt because Jesus asked
him the third time, "Do you love Me?" He said, "Lord,
You know all things; You know that I love [phileo] You..."*
(John 21:15-17).

"Peter was unable to love the Lord with *agape*—the unconditional, highest level of love and devotion. He was grieved because
Jesus had to lower His divine standard of love to accommodate
Peter's weakness. That is how I felt. The brother I had betrayed
lowered the standard of love he had expected from me in order
to accept me and my failure to love him."

A Shepherd's Heart

"Like the prodigal son who yearned to return home, I
expected my father to judge me and revoke my rights as a son.
Just as the prodigal thought he was no longer worthy to be called
a son and was willing to work for his father as a hired servant,
I was willing to do anything (see Luke 15:11-23). But my father
did not give me what I deserved. Though I had wounded him,
he restored all my rights and gave me the best of his inheritance,
with a pure heart. Neither Pastor Jusuf nor Pastor Philip were
like other authoritarian leaders I had known before. They led
me with the heart of a shepherd. As a result, I was free to be
myself, and to become the person God had called me to be. No
longer was I required to serve under pressure from people. I had
never found this freedom under the leaders who left our church.
I finally found shepherds after God's heart (see Ps. 78:70-72).

"I stayed true to my word. When people in the congregation attacked and criticized me, my pastors covered me, assuring them that I had changed. At the risk of their own reputations, they sacrificed themselves for the sake of my resurrection. Their efforts were not in vain. Because they gave me a second chance, my hidden potential was unearthed and ultimately others bore witness to the fruits of my restoration.

"After the church split, Pastor Jusuf asked me not to engage in ministry for at least a month. The purpose of his decision was not that I would be judged, but covered. Afterward, he restored my previous position and promoted me to additional duties as office administrator, chairman of the praise and worship, missions, and prayer ministries, and a satellite church pastor in geographical areas where there was a leadership vacuum, such as in Manado. Their trust restored my self-confidence and the real me. Because of the love and trust of my spiritual fathers, I was transformed from a person ready to lash back and hurt others to one prepared to serve."

Second Chance

"I learned from Pastors Philip and Jusuf's leadership to give second chances to others, regardless if they make serious mistakes. It was their trust in me that ultimately restored me. In turn, they earned my trust, as they have done with many others. That is why I submitted to Pastor Philip when he sent me to Manado, the provincial capital of North Sulawesi between the mountains and the bay.

"Before I left for Manado, I paid my respects to Senior Pastor Jusuf. 'Pastor Jusuf, I will only go to Manado with your blessing.' He blessed me there.

"Even though I preferred not to leave my comfort zone, I went to Manado. Our church in Surabaya was more established and had comfortable facilities. I also had no guarantee of my family's comfort in Manado. But because the Lord and my leaders had asked me to go, I obeyed."

The Call of God

"If the truth be known, long before there was a Mawar Sharon Church in Manado, I heard the voice of the Lord calling me there. He spoke to me in November 2002. At that time, I took no action, but I treasured the Word in my heart.

"But then Benaiah Naresh, a prophet from Malaysia, confirmed the revelation. He prophesied that I would be at Mawar Sharon in Surabaya only until the end of 2003. The following year, I would leave to fulfill my apostolic calling. Shortly thereafter, Pastor Philip appointed me to go to Manado. His decision was a huge leap of faith, considering that I was a core leader at the Surabaya church with many significant responsibilities. For that reason, Pastor Philip's decision surprised many. But I knew that his courage and faith to release me was because he saw the Lord's need. His decision was also a confirmation, as I had never said anything about Manado to anyone.

"Pastor Philip endeavored to walk in God's command that we are to have the mind of Christ (see 1 Cor. 2:16), and not rely on human reasoning. So even if the Lord asked for the best person he had, he would not hesitate to release him at once. He once said privately that the same principle applied to himself. If the Lord ordered him to go somewhere, then he would go, no matter what.

"His courageous faith and my obedience reaped tangible results. By July 2004, just four months after I was installed in Manado, the Mawar Sharon Church there had blossomed rapidly. We had founded five local churches with 2,061 members in Tondano, Tomohon, Bitung, Amurang, and Langowan. God is moving in Sulawesi Island."

Pastor Peter Kaonang's Story

Pastor Peter, 42, is district pastor of the Mawar Sharon churches in Jakarta, West Java, and Kalimantan. I first visited his church in Malang in 2002. Pastor Peter had been a full-time businessman, the owner of a woodcrafts company in Surabaya who left everything behind for the sake of the Lord.

When Pastor Philip asked him to pastor a church in Malang, once he made sure that his wife was in agreement, he sold his house in Surabaya and moved to Malang. That meant leaving his comforts behind to begin a walk of faith. He confided that had he been certain at that point that God called him to be a pastor, that first step of faith would not have been so difficult. But this father of two sons was not confident that he was called to the pastorate, and had doubts that he was the right kind of man for the job.

I asked him why he trusted and obeyed his leader's decision. "What if it turned out that Pastor Philip was wrong? Would you regret having left everything?"

He smiled.

"I know that a father would never purposefully allow his child to fail. If Pastor Philip made the decision, he must have prayed over it carefully. I could have rejected his offer, but I didn't. So it was my decision too, right? Why would I regret it?" he said.

Why I Answered His Call

"Jesus said we are to judge a tree by its fruit (see Matt. 7:16-20). Because I saw the fruit of Pastor Philip's life and ministry, I trusted his decision. I also wanted to learn obedience. Although I didn't fully understand my calling at the time, I took my first step into the ministry purely out of obedience—and it produced fruit.

"It all started one day when Pastor Philip stopped by my workplace to tell me his intention of placing me in Malang. I told him I didn't feel called to that path. He didn't try to persuade me, but asked me to think about it. Sometime later he invited my family to join his family on holiday in Malang.

"I agreed to the vacation, but did not reveal our discussion to my wife. She thought it was just a sightseeing excursion to East Java Province, not far from Surabaya. We visited the city together three times. On the third trip, Pastor Philip pressed me for my final decision.

"This time, I accepted. Although I was well aware of my limitations, I wanted to walk at his level of faith. I had had no formal training and had never preached, but I trusted what the Lord had placed in my leader's heart. I thought that perhaps I had not understood or heard God's voice clearly, so I was content just to follow Pastor Philip's vision.

"During those first few trips, I had asked the Lord, 'If You have called me, please reveal it to my wife.' God answered my prayer. Every time my wife and I went to Malang, I asked her, 'What do you think of this city?'

"She always answered, 'There is something special from the Lord for us here in Malang that we have not found in Surabaya.' She found out about Pastor Philip's invitation later when he talked to both of us about it, and she carried it to God in prayer."

A Heart to Serve

"For the next four months, I made trips back and forth from Surabaya to Malang, leaving Surabaya before dawn. The first task on my to-do list was to stir up prayer among God's people. I asked the full-time ministries at the Mawar Sharon mother church to meet for prayer at 6:15 A.M. The service began at 7 A.M. I felt utterly powerless, so I completely relied on the Lord to help me. I cried out to Him, 'Lord, I cannot do this, but I have the heart for it.'

"Pastor Philip had told me, 'Brother Peter, you have nothing you can boast of as far as the ministry is concerned. But the Lord will empower you to do all things.'

"What he said is true. The Lord does not look for people who are capable and self-sufficient—He looks for those who are willing. I tend to get nervous easily, and to stutter. Yet, the Lord enabled me to lay hold of this ministry and put my confidence in Him, and I know it is all by grace.

"Pastor Philip discipled me closely, and he taught me preaching and other ministerial skills. Ultimately he entrusted greater responsibilities to me in a new field, evangelism. I accepted what my leader said without a direct, personal revelation from the Lord. I was sure that if I submitted to him, wonderful fruit would come forth. So I stepped out in faith. As a result, God has used me to win many souls for Christ.

"I learned much from modeling Pastor Philip's lifestyle—from the way he worked to the way he organized people. By applying his example and his strengths to my ministry, I got good results. I realize that he pays a price for his anointing and that if I continue to seek the anointing of the Lord for my own life, I too will pay a price. But since the day that I set out on this journey of faith, I have never looked back."

My Life Principles

Principle:
Recognize the Boundaries of Fatherhood

> *Even though you have ten thousand guardians in Christ,*
> *you do not have many fathers, for in Christ Jesus I*

became your father through the gospel (1 Corinthians 4:15).

I watch over my spiritual children within the appropriate boundaries. Why do they permit me to intervene in their lives? Because they know I love them and that I would never do anything that is unpleasant for their flesh without a good reason.

I do not plant my life principles in them so they will grow up spiritually to become just like me. Like a proper spiritual father, my job is to make sure my spiritual children can carry their own personal crosses in a way that pleases the Lord. My desire is to see them mature and to know the true calling of God on their lives. I want them to become what God wants them to be. That doesn't mean that they have to become pastors. As long as they follow the Lord and His Word, I will always support them.

When I suggest a rule that constrains their flesh, they never complain. Although they are fully aware of their rights and freedoms, they have never protested or argued with me. Why? Because my spiritual children know I do this with a clear objective and with no hidden agenda.

They obey me because they love the Lord. They know that all I'm doing is to help them find the path to their success. My only task as a spiritual father is to walk alongside them when they must take up their own cross. If they feel blessed by my life and principles, it is because they have learned from me as a living example. As long as they look first to the Lord, and their love and respect for me stays within appropriate limits, never verging on idolatry, they will be edified and established as His disciples.

Because of the demands that my spiritual children put on me, and since I must be an example to them, I train myself to be strong in Christ, for He is the source of my strength. I live out the principle that, as a spiritual father, I must be stronger and more persevering than my children. That way, when they are burdened by trials—conflicts, illness, stagnation, or spiritual decline—looking to the example of their spiritual father encourages them and revives their spirits.

Chapter 10

One Vision, Many Revivals

ARLY in 2003, Pastor Philip had a supernatural encounter with the Lord while he was alone in his bedroom. Jesus came into his room. His presence was so powerful that he lost track of the time. The Holy Spirit urged him to pray, and throughout the visitation, he prayed in tongues, his body trembling greatly in fear. He felt unworthy to receive such a great honor.

As he prayed in the presence of the majestic glory of Jesus, he found that all he could utter was one sentence. That promise, spoken under the anointing, became the core vision for Mawar Sharon Church.

"We will build You 1,000 strong local churches with 1,000,000 disciples."

As soon as the words were out of his mouth, the visitation ended.

In October, as he was relaxing with his wife and daughter, the Holy Spirit spoke to him again.

"Stay awake after your wife and daughter are asleep."

Once his family was sound asleep, he gave himself to prayer, and the Holy Spirit spoke to his heart for five hours. The Lord revealed to him that a great spiritual revival was coming. He felt his spirit lifted outside his body. He saw a tsunami, an unbroken enormous wave swelling hundreds of feet high before him. From behind the waves he heard a voice.

"I will send you a great spiritual revival. It will be very great and you do not know it. In one sweep many souls will be saved."

After he received that promise from the Lord, he went to bed. It was 4 o'clock in the morning.

Holy Ground

Pastor Johannes told me that Pastor Philip's call to help birth revival in his nation was already stirring four years before that visitation in his room.

"The Youth Jamboree in 1999 was the first time we ever saw anything like that. The Lord worked greatly through Pastor Philip." he said.

He and his wife, Lippy, told story after story about the Youth Jamboree, the theme of which was "Be Radical for God." Led by the Holy Spirit, Pastor Philip set apart an area he called "holy ground." That opened the place to a move of God that changed many people's lives. When they mentioned that Pastor Samuel Handoko had a video of the event, I asked to borrow the video and watched it as soon as I could get my hands on it.

Young people from all over Indonesia had thronged to the historic El Bethel Prayer House in Karang Pandan, central Java. Many received the gift of tongues for the first time.

Then Pastor Philip said, "Sanctify this section. This is holy ground. The Lord is in this place. Everyone step back."

People in the front section rolled up their mats and vacated the area. Then the event committee held hands and formed a living fence that barred the empty front section from the Jamboree participants.

"Today let's do something a little different," Pastor Philip said. "Usually the Holy Spirit waits for us to get ready so He can touch us. Let's reverse the order. Let's make our hearts ready before we invite Him to come. Then we will wait for Him. And when the Holy Spirit comes, I want you to come up to the front and touch Him instead of the other way around."

Then he began to sing a worship song

> *Breathe Holy Spirit, in this place*
> *Breathe Holy Spirit, with Your power*
> *Restore Your church in these last days*
> *Breathe, breathe, now.*

The congregation sang the song over and over. Everyone began to pray and sing in tongues. The presence of God was so heavy in that place that many people couldn't stand. They sat on the floor, crying. My heart beat faster as I watched Pastor Philip call people to come forward. They collapsed before arriving at the altar. There were people laughing and weeping everywhere. The presence of God was so powerful that evil spirits shrieked as they came out of some. One person who couldn't stand in His presence crawled his way to the front. Every time he tried to stand up, he failed. He had to gather all his strength to reach the holy ground.

Several people tried to run to the front, but as soon as they set foot on the boundary of the sanctified area, they collapsed in tears. Everyone who entered the holy ground was touched powerfully by God and slain in the Spirit. From time to time, Pastor Philip extended his hands, crying out, "Receive, receive." But the Lord did all the work

An hour passed without my awareness. I was electrified by His presence. I had not gone to the Youth Jamboree five years before, and I didn't know Pastor Philip at that time. Yet I couldn't stop crying. How could I feel His presence so strongly, since the event was long past?

After the Jamboree, many young people surrendered their lives to Jesus and committed to full-time ministry. Pastor Philip prophesied at the event that many of them would be called to leave everything behind for the sake of Christ.

Just as the Lord said, a large number of those young men and women became pastors and planted churches, starting in Salatiga, then Magelang, Semarang, Bandung, and to the four corners of Indonesia. Some of their names are Pastor Yosef

Moro, Pastor Johannes Sonny Susanto, Pastor Danu, and Pastor Bernard Samuel. The lives of these young people were radically changed forever.

> *So the word of God spread. The number of disciples in Jerusalem increased rapidly, and a large number of priests became obedient to the faith* (Acts 6:7).

The Lord Gives the Increase

After the Lord visited Pastor Philip in his room and gave him the vision for revival, he encouraged all of Mawar Sharon's district pastors to hold revival services and crusades. Every month, two major events were planned at the mother church in Surabaya. In June 2004, Mawar Sharon hosted a cell-group conference for all the churches. A few days later, the Festival of God's Power took place in Surabaya. After these two major events, Pastor Philip did not settle down to enjoy the fruit of his labors. Instead, he moved forward aggressively.

I asked him why he didn't slow down his pace.

"If I am the cause of slowing down the speed of God's move, and if it were to cause even one sinner to go further astray, I couldn't bear it. I could never do such a thing," He said.

What more could I say? Perhaps that is why this church never sleeps. Revivals and church-planting are the DNA of spiritual awakening at Mawar Sharon Church.

They Cannot Be Counted

At one point, Pastor Philip claimed that the total church congregation, including the satellite churches, numbered more than 16,000 members. I took the initiative to actually count them because I was almost allergic to the words *around* or *approximately*. I wanted to know the exact figure so I could convince others by publishing the changes at Mawar Sharon Church.

In July 2004, the number of cell-group members from the mother church in Surabaya was 4,447. Added to that were the members of our satellite churches in Surabaya, Sidoarjo, Mojokerto, Malang, Jember, Yogyakarta, Manado, Ambon, Pontianak, and Medan—more than 13,000. The church in Manado was 890, according to Pastor Judy Koesmanto. But as I finalized my count the following week, I learned that the Manado church had already grown to 1,153. I was stunned. What is more, new local churches continued to be pioneered at an accelerated rate. I couldn't get the totals as easily as I'd thought. I had not even begun counting those who were not part of the cell groups. But, I still didn't want to give up, so I continued counting.

Weeks later, I was sure I could wrap up this project once and for all and come up with a final figure. But Pastor Judy burst into my office and shouted happily, "Sianne, guess how big our church in Manado is now?"

I didn't want to speculate, so I answered with the most reasonable figure I could based on the last number he'd given me weeks earlier.

"The congregation must be 1,500," I answered hesitantly.

He smiled with excitement.

"Wrong. That number is too small, Sianne. The church is already 2,061 people."

"What?"

I gave up and stopped counting.

> *I will make your offspring like the dust of the earth, so that if anyone could count the dust, then your offspring could be counted....He took him outside and said, "Look up at the heavens and count the stars—if indeed you can count them." Then He said to him, "So shall your offspring be"* (Genesis 13:16; 15:5).

My Life Principles

Principle 1:
Seeds of Revival: Sow in Tears

> *Those who sow in tears will reap with songs of joy. He who goes out weeping, carrying seed to sow, will return with songs of joy, carrying sheaves with him* (Psalm 126:5-6).

Why doesn't every church experience revival? Why are some churches stagnant while others explode with spiritual growth? Does the Lord show favoritism? Of course not. We should not allow ourselves to be deceived. The Lord is not like us. He is present in every church, and He can work through anyone. Then, since this is true, how do we explain the reason for stagnation?

The answer is simple—we have forgotten to lease our tears to the Lord.

In 2000, during my prayer time, the Lord made a request that at first sounded strange to me.

"Philip, will you lease your tears to Me for the sake of My Church?"

"Why do You want me to lease my tears, Lord?" I asked Him.

"I want your tears to become the seeds of revival," He answered.

"The seeds of revival?" For several moments, I remained silent. Then I answered.

"Yes, Lord. I will lease my tears to You."

From that day on, the Lord has used my tears. I began weeping over souls nearly every night until long past midnight. Those days were the most tiring for me.

Prelude to Revival

In July 2000, the youth congregation at Mawar Sharon numbered only 200. That was a year of great difficulty for everyone. The church had just been through a very painful process of shaking and purification. Many leaders and members had left, resulting in bitterness for a large number of those who stayed. The church had sunk into a deep crisis of trust. But I refused to focus on the setbacks. I trusted in the Lord's promise for this church. I was convinced that at any moment the storm would pass and great joy would break forth in its place. Sustained by the vision the Lord had given me, I resolved to weep for the lost souls and to pray that the empty chairs would soon be filled with new converts. And the Lord saw the sincerity of my heart and my tears.

In just three months, the youth increased rapidly to 600 by October. Though I had not made any move or appeal to the young people to reach out to their friends, every week 15 to 30 new believers were baptized. Without revival services or any effort on the part of the leadership, many non-Christians were converted. That was just the beginning of the move of God—the swells before the tsunami of His revival.

I was astounded. Each time I sowed, I reaped immediate fruit. In fact, eight people accepted Jesus and were baptized the first week after I shed tears for the church. I grew more and more enthusiastic as I witnessed firsthand how the Lord's hand was working mightily for us. Then, in November, we had our inaugural revival service in one of the largest private universities in Surabaya. A visitation from God shook the place. That historic gathering yielded 400 souls in one night.

We held revival services on campuses every week throughout 2001. At one campus, I learned an unforgettable lesson on the ways of the Lord. A cell-group leader from our church came to me after the revival service in tears.

"Pastor, I am so sorry," he said.

I watched him intently, not understanding what he was talking about. He clasped my hand and said between sobs, "All this time I have had negative thoughts about all our church leaders."

I smiled. Now I understood. He had been a church member for a long time, so he had gone through the split and weathered the storm. His heart had been wounded, and it was difficult for him to forget the trauma. He had lost the courage to trust a spiritual leader again, afraid of being disappointed once more.

"I thought you would be the same as those who betrayed us and that you would certainly mislead everyone in the end. But now I trust you."

I threw my arms around him and said, "Don't worry about it. Everything is OK."

When I got home, I searched for data on the cell group the man led. I was surprised to find that his cell group had actually multiplied several times.

"How could a leader struggling with bitterness and anger multiply his cell group so quickly and successfully?" I wondered. "How could a bitter tree bear fruit?" Finally, the Lord opened my eyes to understand His ways. The Lord had overlooked that brother's handicap because He counted my tears (see James 5:15b).

> You number my wanderings; put my tears into Your bottle; are they not in Your book? When I cry out to You, then my enemies will turn back; this I know, because God is for me (Psalm 56:8-9 NKJV).

Principle 2:
Seeds of Revival: Sow in Prayer

During this season, I did not put my hope in any human being, lest I be discouraged. The faith of the young people was extremely fragile. Empty and negative rumors were circulating everywhere. That's not to mention the pessimistic words I heard all around me, which could have crushed my hopes and sown doubt. Sadly, the young people were far from ready to mobilize for the great move of God that was coming.

One day a group of students manifested demonic activity right before my eyes, a result of harboring unforgiveness in their hearts. It was an ugly scene. Their wounded spirits were far from being healed. This reality struck fear in my heart, and I protested to the Lord. "How is it possible for you to use me to have a spiritual revival with people like these? They seem so broken and unable to resist the devil at all, much less help bring about a supernatural breakthrough in this city." I was beginning to lose hope.

"Lord, please do not give me false hopes. Why should I hope for a soul-winning revival? I would be thankful enough just to see these healed of their wounds."

Just as my strength began to fail, the Lord spoke clearly to me. "Philip, you must get up every morning. You must pray."

I thought morning meant 7 A.M. Apparently, I was mistaken. Every day at 1 A.M., the Lord woke me up to pray for souls and to weep for their salvation. The Lord reminded me of the outbreak of spiritual revival in Ungaran through the tears we shed in 1995.

"Philip, do not be afraid. Do you want a revival like the one in Ungaran? Do you want that to happen here in this church? Do you want that to happen in this city?

Through a trickle of my tears I answered, "Of course, I want that, Lord. I want the revival in Ungaran to happen here, too."

Then the Lord revealed to me the restoration of the condition of Zion in His Word (see Neh. 1; Dan. 9:1-19; Heb. 5:7). I prayed for the restoration of Mawar Sharon Church for the next three years. Within six months, our cell groups multiplied from 18 to hundreds. This phenomenal church growth occurred despite the fact that not every cell group had fully recovered from the past trauma. Truly, it was the Lord who restored the condition of this church.

And what happened when the Lord restored the condition of Zion? *Revival.* It was like a dream.

> When the LORD brought back the captives to Zion, we were like men who dreamed. Our mouths were filled with laughter, our tongues with songs of joy. Then it was said among the nations, "The LORD has done great things for them." The LORD has done great things for us, and we are filled with joy. Restore our fortunes, O LORD, like streams in the Negev. Those who sow in tears will reap with songs of joy. He who goes out weeping, carrying seed to sow, will return with songs of joy, carrying sheaves with him (Psalm 126:1-6).

From that day on, no one could dislodge my faith. As soon as our young people saw the unprecedented evidence of a revival, one by one they came to me. Some apologized. Others made bold confessions.

"Pastor Philip, I apologize. Until now, I thought you were a false prophet."

I appreciated their honesty. But I didn't allow myself to be affected by what others thought of me. I knew from the Word of God that the words and opinions of people meant little. What mattered was what the Lord said about me. This commitment was tested constantly. As soon as I mobilized the youth to evangelize the city, many people questioned my leadership. Some harshly criticized me.

"Are you crazy? We should make sure that everyone has been healed first, then mobilize," they said.

But I was determined that I didn't need to wait for everyone to be ready. If no one was willing to walk with me for the sake of revival, I would still go on walking. If necessary, I would weep alone with Jesus until I saw them grow.

One by one, people mobilized to help carry the Lord's burden. They became mightily moved to weep for souls. Every morning I called out their names in prayer before the Lord (see Exod. 28:11-12; 29).

"Prepare them Lord. Prepare them."

I determined not to focus on the problem, but to set my vision on revival. Every prayer was saturated in faith.

"Give me Surabaya or I'll die."

The Lord answered my prayers and petitions. The spiritual condition of the youth changed drastically. The fire of the Holy Spirit was raging in the church. God's visitation was real in every service. Everyone began evangelizing. We scheduled revival services, and the results were beyond our expectations. From 2002 to 2004, local churches were established everywhere. The congregation increased as we reached thousands of disciples for Christ.

News about the spiritual revival spread far and wide. The Lord caused a great stir in people's hearts everywhere. It was as if a current of high-voltage electricity resurrected the spiritually dead. Men and women alike were suddenly awakened from their long spiritual sleep. People shouted in astonishment, *"The LORD has done great things for them"* (Ps. 126:3).

Today, God is still moving at Mawar Sharon Church. The fire of our revival keeps burning, fueled by holy discontent until the day we welcome the coming of Christ.

Let me ask you a question. Do you want to see revival in your life and in your church? Then become a partner with Jesus Christ in Gethsemane. Wrestle in prayer until revival comes. Press through as you pray. Pray until a breakthrough bursts forth. Pray for lost souls. Come with a humble heart; kneel and say, "Lord, I long to see an even greater spiritual revival in this place. I desire a visitation of God for every soul."

The Lord called me to lease my tears to Him. Now He is calling you to do the same.

Pastor Jusuf Soetanto and family

Partners in life and ministry

Family picture in Bali

Entrance and lobby area at Mawar Sharon Church, Surabaya

Worship service at Mawar Sharon Church, Surabaya

Sea of young people dancing and praising the Lord at an outdoor
revival service called "Victory," September 19-20, 2008.

An unforgettable encounter with Jesus.
The Festival of God's Power, June 8-9, 2007, Jatim Expo, Surabaya

The sky witnessed wonders of God: 3,946 people responded to the altar call and 812 of them were immediately baptized that night at the Book of Life crusade, April 11-12, 2008, Surabaya.

Asia for Jesus
A vision as big as the continent of Asia

Army of God
52,000 people packed the runway of Juanda International Airport-Surabaya on May 14-16, 2009. As many as 4,246 unbelievers accepted Christ and 1,252 people were baptized during that historical event.

The Airport Miracles
Tens of thousands received the Pentecostal gift of tongues simultaneously for the first time.

Pastor Philip with Asia for Jesus family and friends

Mawar Sharon Church in Bandung

Mawar Sharon Church in Medan

Mawar Sharon Church in Jakarta

Mawar Sharon Church in Sidoarjo

Mawar Sharon Church in Semarang

Mawar Sharon Church in Manado

Mawar Sharon Church in Salatiga

Mawar Sharon Church in Jogiakarta

Mawar Sharon Church in West Surabaya

Mawar Sharon Church in Malang

Mawar Sharon Church in Bali

Praying in a public place for the salvation of Taipei after they joined the Evangelism Conference "Taiwan for Jesus" in February 2007.

Youth in Taiwan took revival to the street.

"The Five Brothers" (from left to right): Pastor Ewen Chow, Pastor Timothy Yen, Pastor Philip Mantofa, Pastor Jonathan Chow, Pastor Jaeson Ma

Praying for Asia

God touched many nations in Asia.

A woman was healed miraculously by God at the Festival of God's Power in Taipei, Taiwan, February 13-14, 2008

Thousands of people filled the stadium of National Taiwan University. Multitudes of souls received Christ for the first time during the altar call.

"I believe in miracles, for I believe in God!"

"Let the devil be ashamed when he sees this!"

About Philip Mantofa

PASTOR Philip Mantofa graduated in theology from Columbia Bible College, British Columbia, Canada. Since 1998, he has been serving in Mawar Sharon Church, a growing church of 30,000 in Indonesia. Currently, he is the assistant head of Gereja Mawar Sharon denomination, which has a network of 70 local churches. Since his younger age, he has brought more than 100,000 souls to Christ. His passion is to ignite the fire within the younger generation to become pastors and spiritual leaders all around Asia. Moreover, he has a burning desire to see nations experience and encounter the love of Jesus Christ. He is happily married to Irene Saphira with three lovely children: Vanessa, Jeremy, and Warren

IN THE RIGHT HANDS, THIS BOOK WILL CHANGE LIVES!

Most of the people who need this message will not be looking for this book. To change their lives, you need to put a copy of this book in their hands.

> *But others (seeds) fell into good ground, and brought forth fruit, some a hundred-fold, some sixty-fold, some thirty-fold* (Matthew 13:8).

Our ministry is constantly seeking methods to find the good ground, the people who need this anointed message to change their lives. Will you help us reach these people?

> *Remember this—a farmer who plants only a few seeds will get a small crop. But the one who plants generously will get a generous crop* (2 Corinthians 9:6).

**EXTEND THIS MINISTRY BY SOWING
3 BOOKS, 5 BOOKS, 10 BOOKS, OR MORE TODAY,
AND BECOME A LIFE CHANGER!**

Thank you,

Don Nori Sr., Publisher
Destiny Image
Since 1982

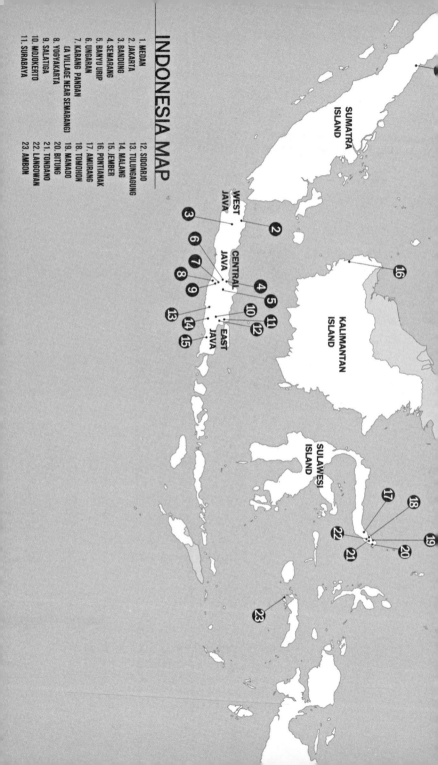

INDONESIA MAP

SUMATRA ISLAND

KALIMANTAN ISLAND

SULAWESI ISLAND

WEST JAVA

CENTRAL JAVA

EAST JAVA